D1517919

Outside the Walls

Books by Vassilis Vassilikos

The Plant, the Well, the Angel
Z
The Photographs
The Harpoon Gun
Outside the Walls

Outside the Walls

VASSILIS VASSILIKOS

Translated from the Greek by MIKE EDWARDS

HARCOURT BRACE JOVANOVICH, INC., NEW YORK

73223
NORTH BABYLON PUBLIC LIBRARY

Copyright © 1973 by Vassilis Vassilikos

All rights reserved. No part of this publication may be
reproduced or transmitted in any form or by any means,
electronic or mechanical, including photocopy, recording,
or any information storage and retrieval system,
without permission in writing from the publisher.

ISBN 0-15-170515-1

Library of Congress Catalog Card Number: 72-88795

Printed in the United States of America

First edition

B C D E

To Mimi

Contents

Outside the Walls

Inside the Walls

Ah why didn't I observe them when they were building the walls?
. . .
Imperceptibly they shut me out of the world.

> —C. P. Cavafy, "Walls"
> Translated by Rae Dalven

The confines of the walls, starting from Koraï Street, including the whole of Syntagma Square, ascending Queen Sophia Avenue to embrace Kolonaki and Dexameni Squares, stopping at the approaches to Mount Lycabettus, and including a sliver of Maraslion, constitute one of the central sectors of Athens. Since, in the construction sense, there are no actual walls, their demarcation is not absolute, several offices below Koraï Street also belonging within, as well as a quite considerable section of Plaka, while Omonia Square, the Acropolis, the Hilton, and Truman's statue remain definitely outside. The reader, with his "what doesn't belong" to the walls, may thus trace for himself their imaginary locus.

My motive for writing about these walls lies in the fact that the whole of Greece is adjudged and directed from within their boundaries. When we consider that Palace, chamber, Ministries, residences of premiers, past and present, theaters, cinemas, newspaper chains, airlines, tourist offices, et cetera, all fall inside the walls, it's no exaggeration to say that the heart of the heart, the state of the state, the life of life itself is regulated by them. The primary aspiration for all who live inside is to get outside. The primary ambition for those who live outside is to get inside.

To all appearances the walls are closed to no one. All day long people come and go through their gates. Yet beneath this surface the walls are well and truly shut, the gates as impassable as museum doors after hours. The inmates live a life of their own which no outsider can penetrate. They have their own haunts and

3

hangouts, their own homes in which to spend their evenings, and above all their own language, by no means easy for an intruder to understand.

Let the reader not imagine it to be a question of class distinction. Within the walls live many lowly day laborers. Others claim that even if fate has decreed they live inside the walls they really belong on the outside. The worst of it is that the walls don't acknowledge such exemptions. Whosoever lives within the walls, like it or not, belongs to them, constitutes one of their organic members: he's a single die in their, to outsiders, singular mosaic.

Life within the walls is hard. Lots of housing under construction, lots of traffic in circulation. For cabdrivers, a fare inside the walls is a veritable martydom, never exceeding ten drachmas. Not that the streets are narrow, but so many cars parked to right and left— "What sort of government is this?" expostulate the cabbies—render traffic flow problematical. Wealth abounds within the walls. So for someone with no money, like myself, exasperation is permanent, hanging ever imminent on the tip of the tongue. Yet, like me, there are many others living within the walls without exactly knowing they do, because the walls, as I have said, are really invisible.

Many whose fates have ordained they should live outside arrive daily to announce their "present," punching their invisible time clock at the walls' grilled window. For the walls' inhabitants have a habit of forgetting quickly. When they can't see you, for them you cease to exist. And since careers are carved out within the walls, for one pursuing a career, be it positive or negative—a frequent appearance within becomes essential—because doing nothing is another form of career.

The walls are no dispatch office for sundry concerns: they are no waiting room. The walls are the prime concern: they are the chamber of operations. Hence the curse of the walls is that they lead nowhere and never return to the world what they steal from it. All they produce is printed matter in the form of commemorations, critiques, prizes, or some small monetary tidbit. The walls absorb life, pulp it, and, under a motley of masks, recycle it. Hence the forgery, the fraudulence, the despoliation, the lack of every organic link between our people and their mouthpieces in the theater, cinema, politics, and literature.

There also exist dramatic cases of people for whom a visit inside the walls constitutes the event of the week, even of the month. Living outside, they await important decisions from within. I don't mean those who come to submit an application or a memo, to see an art exhibition or a fine theatrical production. I have in mind those whose product depends on the opinion of the people of the walls, for whom recognition by the latter constitutes the major milestone in their lives because deep down they want to belong inside the walls, to mount their highest ramparts. Every so often the rope breaks, the rope ladder snaps, or is made to snap by someone whose arrival elsewhere is equivalent to his own displacement, as space within is stiflingly restricted. At least I and others like me, living inside the walls, don't gaze upon them as the famished do upon manna in the wilderness; we expect nothing of them, nothing other than their downfall. In any case, I well recall my adolescent years in Salonika when a trip down to Athens was the event of the year for me, and the renewal of my acquaintance with the people of the walls—the same then as now—kept me going for the remaining months. Nowadays I note the same in former townspeople of mine visiting Athens, whom I meet wandering the walled streets. How avidly they crave news—news?—how deep down they envy me, despite all show of sympathy, the privilege of living within the walls, of having connections and contacts on the inside.

The walls, as I have said, stem not from class roots. There are all sorts of apples in the barrel. But in recent years serious inroads have been made by tourists. I don't mean the hordes that flock in and out during the summer; rather, foreigners cast up from the shores of their own societies coming to rent homes inside the walls because, as they say, "there's more happening here." Indeed, many of these scrawny creatures or bearded brigands may well be agents for their countries, preferring the walls because only from here can they extract secrets. But then, they may simply be artists, in which case they consort with the walls' more jaded inmates.

Of course, there are walls within the walls: those people—as a rule overly refined beings, who've spent a considerable portion of their lives abroad—who are unable to bear the "square" outlook of the walls' residents make up a tighter circle, just as the corona around Salonika's White Tower forms a minor tower. This elite exerts every effort to crack the walls, forgetting, however, that outside exists a population of 8 million people for whom the walls are already inaccessible. So the walls within the walls weave around and around in a vicious circle, the voices from within tuned to receivers sensitive to limited frequencies, penetrating not even the outer walls' prescribed boundaries. These inmost inmates do have a safety valve against asphyxia, for with a short trip abroad— having funds at their disposal from legacies, et cetera—they can breathe real European air, recuperate, and return more determined than ever to crush the walls.

The walls, or, more precisely, the people of the walls, move with the seasons. They've developed common tastes and partialities, so you may see a considerable portion of their population on Hydra at Easter, and in the summer on Mykonos or Skyros, or at Pelion. There they raise around themselves the same "high and mighty" walls and, though they insist they're summering, despite etesian breezes and cool Aegean mistral, their lungs inhale the self-same fetid air. The people of the walls have learned to live exclusively among their own kind, so much so that even their wounds can be salted only by others from within. To them, an insult from an outsider is no insult; it's a divertissement. They relish his insanity. In other words it's a question of habit, much the same as hashish. Woe unto them that fling not their windows wide to the outside world. They'll freeze one day and die of pleurisy when new winds blow.

The walls provide security. With what delight I roam their

streets, despite the risk of falling scaffold poles or squealing tires, but how insecure I feel in a quiet, deserted neighborhood, in Kaisariani or Aigaleo. There they'll devour me: there live grim-faced ghouls. Here they devour me and I don't care. Inside the walls, behind a mask of calmest connivance, are perpetrated the vilest crimes.

From time to time the walls body forth a new face that becomes known overnight throughout Greece. This face must belong to a cadaver, because the walls' moribund savings bank thrives on necrology. A clean and healthy organism interests the people of the walls only insofar as it displays the likelihood of its decay. If there seems no such possibility, it's all clear, as they say, to "get the hell out of here." Corruption is the law of the walls, though all maintain that is precisely what they oppose. Cadavers from the provinces in particular interest the walls. Cadavers or near cadavers pass more easily through the meat grinder. Yet if some personage inside the walls makes his mark outside, that is, wins fame abroad, his first task is to swagger about the walls that have nurtured him. Within the walls snobbery constitutes the rule. Suicides constitute the exception. That snobbery is law I've seen with my own eyes on Good Friday. People were sitting at outdoor patisseries eating sweetmeats as Saint Dionysios' Epitaphios procession was passing. "What's going on?" I inquired. "Can't you see?" came the retort. "They're doing the Epitaphios Strut."

Now and then, popular manifestations take place inside the walls. Pre-election meetings, demonstrations, protests. The gates open and a sea of people floods the neighboring squares and streets. Yet those who speak, those up there behind the microphones, are people from inside the walls, people who have no connection with the masses. Not in theory, not in practice, for they live within.

But there are also those living outside who dream daily of the walls, communicate by telephone with the inmates, base their every expedition on prior consultation. These, too, are sad cases. They remind me of those minor keeps in the Middle Ages whose every move was subject to the central feudal castle. In place of messengers there are now telephones. Meanwhile, outside the walls, the people go on tilling an earth never their own until they die.

Death for others is life for the walls. Of course, all maintain the contrary. All rest their eyes, their expectations, their hopes on the masses. But the masses have no connection with those within because the inmates, as individuals, live a life all their own. Whatever differences may set them apart, a stronger bond unites them: they live inside the walls.

You'll see nothing more incongruous than the construction workers on their break sprawled across the sidewalk basking in the sun, or eating, bespattered with whitewash, in the tavernas, or hurrying to catch the afternoon bus to get home to their own neighborhoods. Within the walls they look like bizarre birds, birds of some other squall, come here to roost in the branches of this odious, immured realm. They're so much alive that the scaffolding beside them looks fake. They don't know that building houses fortifies the walls. If they did, they would not refuse to build them, but they would at least try to make them flimsier, so that at the first opportunity they themselves would be back to demolish them.

I believe a time will come when these invisible walls that so very perceptibly shut out the rest of the world will be abolished, with Spanish dirges and founts of blood from wounded whales.

One

Cleanthis, the Guild
of Ragpickers

As of April 15 the disposal of refuse in the central sector of
Athens will be effected by special new refuse vehicles, of which
the Municipality of Athens is shortly to take delivery. These
vehicles are equipped with a complete internal system of refuse
absorption, so as to eliminate the unsavory spectacle currently
presented by the regular garbage trucks.

—Newspaper story

While these declarations on the part of His Worship the Mayor
signified for all of us a mark of civilization and progress, one
special class of people was left grieving: people who live on what
we discard, people who have done the same job for years, for whole
decades, people for whom the mills—"mills" are what they call
the new vehicles the municipality is to introduce—are tantamount
to a death sentence.

Here's what's actually happening: beyond Ano Liosia, where
the lined asphalt ends and you hit the dirt road, to the right of the
Athens–Corinth railway track, lies the Athens Municipal Garbage
Dump. It's an open site, a flat tract between the mountains, facing
the ever-shimmering Skaramanga sea. Here a succession of municipal trucks arrives to dump their garbage. A bulldozer levels it off.
Then another, yellow, brand-new, a little longer, covers it with dirt
and grinds over it like a steam roller. Thus, in time, this elastic
platform came into being. And thus, gradually, it will span the
entire cleft that once separated the two mountains. It's high noon,
peak traffic, and the sun vertical.

When one of the municipal trucks comes to unload, the ragpickers know exactly what it's bringing and from which neighbor-

hood of Athens. Even before it heaves into sight, they can tell its number from the very sound of its engine. If it's downwind and its engine is inaudible, its canopy has but to appear at the end of the road and they can identify it. They prepare the reception according to the truck. Any and every squabble hinges on who'll get first grab. They quarrel, curse, shove like a mob at a bus terminal. Right from the dump entry it's pursued by a rushing disorderly rabble until it lurches to a halt. Even before the garbage hits the dust, they swoop on it, plunge into it, and burrow for a while in its heaps. Then they emerge, shaking a shower of garbage from their heads and shoulders, each proudly clutching his booty. A girl, dressed like a man, carts off a fat stiff cat. A man hauls away a bedspring. Two or three others abscond with gas canisters. Yet others clutch handfuls of scraps—salami or sausages or the odd orange in season—heading for the water supply to wash them. But here human logic draws the line of distinction from the law of the jungle. Whatever each has grabbed is now his and his alone. Nobody argues about that. There's no case of what you see in the Royal Gardens when you toss a dry crust to the squawking ducks, one snatching it from the beak of the other. No. Here the only strife takes place beforehand. Then it's each to his own fate, though, let me add, the battle for the cream of the garbage is quite short and sweet. The first bulldozer, biding its time, intervenes with its forethrust soon after the dumping and distributes the garbage all around "in equal shares of tenderness." Then more ragpickers arrive, these lacking the contentious disposition of the others, and more calmly, almost at their leisure, begin sifting.

"The plushest garbage," one of them told me, "comes from Kolonaki and the Central Market. Kolonaki brings in good swabs and plenty of paper, as well as a lot of valuables. But those mostly get pinched on the way by the drivers. They keep their eyes peeled, too. From the Central Market you get bones, fruit, vegetables, and skins. There's a truck we call 'hard meat,' brings just bones, by the sackful. If you catch that one, you make fifteen or twenty drachs, easy."

A good many vault up on the open trucks while they're still going full tilt. First they clamber up behind the trailer, then with a bound they're inside. So by the time they reach the dumping spot the bounders have already had first choice. A young lad scrambles down a newly dumped load with a sheaf of rods for booty.

In contrast, the elderly squat cross-legged, each by his own heap of garbage, sifting it like lentils with rakelike hands. Stones and other foreign bodies they set to one side.

It's hard to distinguish the women from the men as they circle around in patched pants and tattered shirts, smoking and screeching in strident tones like harpies out of hell.

Children assist the grownups. An entire society shelters in shacks that look like chicken coops—fit, you'd think, for anything but human habitation. And yet . . .

Shocks are many and great for the stranger coming here, like me, for the first time. First of all, it's hard to believe that just fifteen kilometers outside our sweet tourist city exists this dark age of human exploitation. Even if you shut your eyes and block your ears and tell yourself, "I'm not here, it's someone else," the smell, an unbearable stench, will constantly remind you that you are in this place, you and none other, and around you are people reduced to ratlike vermin, living permanently in, off, and for garbage.

Thrice I went, thrice I saw, and thrice I could not overcome my shame before this prodigy of human degradation. And the people who took me, different each time, all experienced the same symptoms as I: nausea, depression, compunction, guilt. And thrice the sun made the Skaramanga sea shimmer like a mirage in the wilderness. In every home, trash barrels are just one domestic problem, especially for apartment buildings whose residents have agreed among themselves not to put their garbage outside their doors until the minute the janitor rings from below. Always a rancid odor lingers. With such hypersensitivity, imagine what the garbage dump is like. After each of our visits we washed, changed our clothes, sheets, shoes, and above all tried to forget. But the ragpickers remain, victims of our hypersensitivity conserved in its hot-houses in the name of the dung we shower on others.

"But don't they catch anything? Don't they get sick?" I asked a man who looked like one of the boss's employees.

"Listen," he replied, with not a hint of cynicism, "I'm firmly convinced, after several months working here, there are no germs. Just a few feeble organisms. Take these people—they never catch a thing. They eat whatever they dig out of the garbage and they're all in fine shape. A few days back one of the trucks brought in some fifty frozen chickens thrown out by the medical officer as unfit for the market. This lot had a feast. Split 'em in half, lit fires, roasted 'em, then ate 'em. Sometimes they get cuts. Catch hold of bits of glass, or paper wrapped round razor blades. They bleed. Nothing . . ."

I take a hurried stroll around where they're sifting garbage, try-ing to breathe as little as possible. My friend, camera in hand, is like a "stab in the eye" to the ragpickers. All turn their faces away in shame. This is no job, they think, for the world to see us doing. And if some acquaintance happens to recognize them? Several get angry and threaten us. Only one mutters, as we pass, with a touch of irony and sorrow, "Take a picture, buddy, to show the King."

A spool of coffee-colored film enmeshed in the garbage like the slough of a snake suddenly sets me pondering what would happen if someone brought a movie camera to shoot scenes of life on the garbage heap. Of course the film would be banned by the censor, but I wonder whether some shots mightn't pass for scenes from concentration camps for Jews. Heaps of old shoes. Spectacle frames. Rotting clothes. Baskets of stale crusts for the pigs. Mangled baby carriages. Rusted wall faucets. Old iron. Bicycle tires. A doll's pink head, its eyes wide with amazement. Still intact, a forty-five-r.p.m. record of a song called "Society My Judge." Bundles of paper ready for disposal. Heaps of small cans: margarine, BP, tomato purée, preserves. A shack constructed from contractors' and civil engi-neers' signboards, with a plaque on the side: KTEL STOP NO. 4. And the drone of the bulldozer, solitary cicada in this purgatory, sustaining bass to the chorus of human protestation.

I stop to question a ragpicker sporting a threadbare overcoat from my grandmother's day.

"If you call this livin', you're crazy," he answers. "We live in mortal sin."

"Where's your home?"

"In the Peristeri slums. But I only go there weekends. Rest of the week I stay here, in them shacks."

"What d'you earn?"

"Depends. Sometimes twenty, sometimes forty a day. We've got a good boss now. He don't rob us when we weigh up like the ones before."

A goat roams about nibbling whatever she can find. Two dogs have lost their bark. Hens strut from the human chicken coops. And the people, bent double, searching, searching. A constant stream of new trucks arriving. Some run, some have had enough. After all, what they find isn't theirs. The overseer will take it from them. So why wear themselves out more? It'll do just to find a bite to eat to keep from starving. Meanwhile the smell's become intolerable. It's completely enveloped me, saturated my clothes like fog. I feel sick.

In the Small Cheer refreshment parlor, sole airtight shack in the area, I seek refuge from the stench. I'm soon joined by the boss, a stocky man with a mustache, who at first eyes me with suspicion, though, once convinced of the integrity of my intentions, isn't slow to pour out his heart.

"Coffee?"

I couldn't taste a thing. "No, thanks."

He obliges me by explaining the whole system of contracting: this site belongs by right to the Municipality of Athens. It operates "by license from the Ministry of Social Welfare and the Sanitary Center of Attica." The municipality tenders the lease to those interested in working it. He himself took a six-month lease, for

60,000 drachmas a month, which is to say, rain or snow, he pays city hall 2,000 a day. "And as it's rained and snowed a lot this year, business is bad. I'm out of pocket. . . ." One of the municipality's obligations is the overlaying of the garbage. For this purpose there are two bulldozers. One scatters, the other smothers. After the overlay the garbage is sprayed with *diazino*, a strong and costly insecticide—140 drachmas per kilo. By this means the site is protected against bacteria. For all these tasks the municipality has eight employees, six on the bulldozers and two supervisors.

"And the rest work for you?"

"No," he replies. "Alas, no. As things stand, there's no labor contract. Each man's his own boss. And I'm nobody's. Ragpickers are a special class of people, kind of bohemian. They can't stand pressure. They come to work when they feel like it. When they don't, they don't. One'll come at six o'clock in the morning, another at ten. And they stop whenever they feel like it. When the weather improves, a lot'll leave, take up peddling around the suburbs, or selling fish. Come the cold, they congregate here. So business booms in winter. About a hundred come altogether. But this year it's been really cold. They'd just come and sit in this place, drinking. 'Get out and work,' I tell 'em. 'Why should we?' they say. 'I'm losing money.' 'What's that to us?' they say. Pissed out of their minds. A lot of them are no-good bums, just envious. Happy to see you bankrupt. 'So why should you wear a tie and not us?' they say. But there are a lot of family men among 'em, too, with families in Kato Liosia, Saint Meletia, Kokkinia, or Aigaleo. They come here to work, to earn an honest day's pay. They're people you can come to terms with. A couple of old boys from Epirus have already bought a small house plot with their earnings, as well as a truck trailer they live in to avoid paying rent."

"How many living here?"

"Some forty families. They live here because they don't have anywhere else to go."

"How d'you pay them?"

"According to what they collect. They bring the stuff to me, we weigh it in front of 'em, then I pay 'em. There are fixed rates. Forty lipta per oka of bone. That's about two kilos. Thirty per oka paper. Half a drach per oka glass. One drach per oka rag. Then I load up my two trucks and send it all to factories as raw material. Bones to the chemical plants. Shoes to the brick kilns. But shoes they won't sell me. A tanner takes 'em at two drachs more. They keep whatever else is profitable, too. The one thing they mustn't do is take off the site such items as I buy myself. And you have to be all smiles and sweetness with 'em, kid gloves, because they're a temperamental lot. The other day they had a hell of a squabble over a gold sovereign. Someone saw it. But a woman stepped on it. He was claiming it was his. She, it was hers. Then it was insult for insult. The woman's husband storms over. He takes her part. Demands the sovereign. The other makes out he's swallowed it. Punches, blows, slaps in the face to make him puke it up. So I rush over. Go to separate them. Catch it from both sides. In the end the other man agrees to split it. He hands it over to me. Naturally he hadn't swallowed it. When I saw it, I could've cried. It was a plastic sovereign, for a New Year's cake."

A driver interrupts the boss with something about the loading. The boss goes off with him. Once I'm alone, the woman serving says, "There'll never be another boss like him set foot here. Impossible. Heart of gold. Six months we've had him now. . . ."

Outside once more I start asking questions. The majority avoid me. I catch one or two expert glances scanning my jacket, my shoes, future rag for industry. From rich industrialists down to raw-material gatherers I see, as in Jacob's dream, an endless ladder vanishing into the heavens, myself on one of the middle to lower rungs, teetering from lack of balance. Even prison must be better than this, I reflect, despite the foul effluvia from the buckets in the prisoners' cubicles. I look at my jacket and recall the words of a ragpicker: "Greece is a poor country. What can you expect from her garbage? Only when they've picked up an oka of cholera does a Greek throw out his clothes." Now they avoid me. There's no greater shame than for human beings to be ashamed of having been born human. Their gaze lacks luster, like the murky retsina they drink in the Small Cheer. In place of eyelashes they have barbed wire, like the Jews. Only when I blurt out I'm a journalist —which I'm not—that I'm concerned for their welfare, do they stand and waver, a dull hope in their eyes. Their amazement at my "concern" is greater even than this hope.

"We're dying of TB," says one. "We're slowly roasting, but may our children live."

"I used to be a carter for the council and the bosses," an old man tells me outside his shack, a big yellow pimple on his cheek. "Twenty years now I've done this job. Better a ragpicker than a scavenger. Twenty years and I'll come out with not a penny pension. The old bosses were racketeers. Robbed us blind, along with the profiteers. Seventy okas we'd weigh up for 'em, twenty they'd pay us for. This boss's all right. But what's the use? Soon it'll be the mills—the new municipal trucks—and they'll destroy us."

From all around rise voices of protest:

"The mills'll be the death of us."

"We'll starve with the mills."

"The mills'll pound the garbage into flour."

"They'll grind it up like meat in prewar mincers."

"Now the garbage comes in good shape."

"Now we eat. The best oranges, salami, in summer fresh cucumber and tomatoes. With the mills we'll eat nothing. They'll make it all into one gooey mass. Pulp. Pap. There's already about ten of these trucks, and we know—not a crumb escapes."

"The mills are German," says Uncle Mitsos, an old boy with a long mustache. "Remember '41. We were at war with Germany; it's Germany they're bringing back. They're German trucks. So what else do we eat? Did we ever see oil? It all goes to the Americans and the English. Seed oil for us."

"That's what His Worship the Mayor does for us."

"I'm not ashamed to work in garbage," Uncle Mitsos continues, raising his voice. "But I'd be ashamed to turn shyster. Forty years I've been in this trade. I've worked, praised be the Almighty, on all the dumps. In those days the council didn't have but one truck. The rest were carts. And what didn't they bring! Even dead horses, what we'd skin the hides off and sell. But nowadays the world's gone in for *civilicizatin*. Now even the ABC's they teach in school they never taught in them days. Me, as I stand here, I got two girls, one grown up, one sixteen. I wouldn't send them into a factory on into the street. The oldest I sent to school. She learned all the thirty-six letters of the alphabet, but she couldn't find a job nowhere. All 'come back tomorrow, come back tomorrow.' So I go to the deputy. He just says 'we'll see.' In the end he had the janitor tell me the Right Honorable Deputy's not home. So I decided grammar gets you nowhere, so my youngest should go in for hairdressing. The poor girl keeps on at me: 'Daddy, why don't you change your job?' 'The job's nothing to be ashamed of,' I tell her. 'But it's shameful to be a shyster.' "

"Uncle Mitsos is a riot," says someone nearby. "No substitute. He'll rap on for two hours solid and you won't get bored."

"What about rain?" I ask.

"God chucked down snow, we'd still pick up the odd bone, a bit of paper. . . ."

Suddenly a man of medium build with bright intelligent eyes appears. Topped with a fur cap, he's introduced as president of the Athens Guild of Ragpickers, Cleanthis. His presence quiets the rest, and they rally around him.

"Our life is a charade," the president begins.

"We're treated worse than garbage," someone shouts, but those around him cover his mouth to allow the president to speak.

"The state has utterly abandoned us," he continues. "We're only good for the army or for our votes. Otherwise, the state ignores us. So much clothing from abroad, and they give us nothing. Most of us were born in garbage, and in garbage we've grown old. Wherever the garbage goes we go, we set up our shacks. We know no other trade. Our wages are starvation wages. We fall sick and if we can, we pay; if we can't, we rot or die. Our guild numbers 150 enrolled and fifty not yet enrolled. Our principal demand is for insurance under the Social Security Plan. The Ministry of Labor gave a favorable reply to our application. And the plan itself will raise no objection. But our employers, present ones excepted, will oppose it. They'll try to prevent insurance for us. It's not in their interest. They have the money, they have the means. We have nothing. Only a just cause. And disease. Each of us has at least one or two. Bronchitis or chronic rheumatism, as a rule."

"I haven't got anything, Mr. John," protests a woman from the crowd.

"Ever had a doctor examine you?"

"No."

"So we beseech you," the president resumes, "do whatever's in your power to let our voice be heard. Speak for us. We want Social Security. It's life or death to us. It's a crime we should be left to die like this."

A jet leaves its white vapor trail across the sky. Tomorrow the latest moon rocket is to be tested, so the papers say.

Mr. Paul Kapasubabo, diplomat from Leopoldville, and Mr. Chung Kun Kim, diplomat from Seoul, have arrived and are staying, the former at the King George Hotel, and the latter at the King Melathron. Mr. Donald Naylor, London shipowner . . .

"One time, at the Petrakis dump," ventures one of them, encouraged by the presence of the president, "some cops got on our tail. The reason was the council hadn't leased the dump to any contractor, so they posted cops to guard it. The sergeant—'Coco' we nicknamed him, because he looked like a clown—says, 'Can't you take a piece of advice, you guys? I said no stealing.' 'What are we stealing? It's our bread and butter, this is. We only came so we won't starve.' 'It's prohibited.' And he sets the bulldozer ready to bury us. We just keep poking around. Then Coco yells, 'Stop in the name of the law or I'll shoot.' And they surround us. 'I'll have you court-martialed for this.' They took a couple of guys and held 'em in detention to make an example. We beat it down the slope. . . ."

Injustice is throttling these people like a noose around their necks, just as a similar noose, the stench of the garbage dump, is throttling me. I move off. A host of thoughts, of questions still unanswered in this jungle of self-interest: with the new trucks the municipality is introducing will there be anyone equipped to take care of these people? Will the boss see they're insured so only one enemy, hunger, remains? And the employer who succeeds this one, will he be honest or will he rob them like his predecessors? Why doesn't the municipality take them into its employ, like the eight who overlay the garbage? Or is the overlaying all we are ever concerned with? For those who still doubt the truth of what I write, I have but one suggestion: go see for yourselves. You can't miss it. After Three Bridges you keep seeing municipal trucks on their way back, canopies raised. Then to the right of the railway track you hit the dirt road. Rags and paper, caught on the wild thyme and scrub on the flank of the naked hill, gleam like whitecaps on the spuming sea. Then the smell will compel you to roll up the windows. In back, the sea.

On the way home, against the other background, high on the holy rock rears the skeleton of the Parthenon, imperishable symbol of Greek civilization.

A Village

The village stands on an island close to Albania. Its geographical location is of no importance. It could be anywhere in Greece and what follows hold equally true, as could its café—a café like any other, with tables and chairs, a sticky strip like a tie, for catching flies, in the middle where the electric light bulb ought to hang, except that the village, like so many villages, has no current. On the walls, advertisements for Sissy milk, Fix, "the Beer of Olympic Champions," Matsangou cigarettes; a photo of His Majesty in his youth, smiling; a picture of a ship foundering in heavy seas. And from the Bureau of Public Information, large panels with photos of the War of Independence and the April 4 NATO Day celebrations, bearing such legends as, "Under the aegis of peace and security afforded by her membership in NATO, Greece is making steady advances. She merits them. Tractors and a thousand and one other machines replace oxen while . . ." and, "The sacred tree of Greek liberty is unwithering," and, "We the Greeks of today, inspired by the immortal example of the heroes of 1821, honor the eternal Hellenic principles Fatherland—Religion—Family as we build a richer and more powerful Greece." Farther on, the price list, an advertisement for "Beauteous Greece," a notice that the hotel in town is "resuming functions completely renovated," and in bold handwritten characters, "Communism = Treason = Infamy = Blood." "Constantine Canaris sets fire to the flagship of the Turkish fleet under the command of Kapoutan Pasha, June 18, 1822."

The café is under the command of Uncle Demos, an old but hale and hearty, hard-of-hearing ex-skipper of sail. His right hand is his grandson Plutarch, a sharp-witted boy of twelve, dashing about with plates and dishes, since the café is also a restaurant and, on the top floor, a hotel. Guests include an apprentice agriculturalist and a peasant woman from a neighboring rock island here to have her daughter treated for a bowel infection. The village has a resident doctor who receives, as inscribed on his name plate, "daily when in attendance all who dwell within his practice." Each morning lines of peasants wait outside his scantily stocked surgery. The thousand ailments they suffer have recently been augmented by one more, induced by parathion, a toxin used for spraying olives against caries, one lungful of which is enough to grab your stomach.

Also staying on the top floor are a retired bank clerk and his wife, come from "town" for sand baths. He styles himself bourgeois. "The open air affects us bourgeois," he grumbles. The café overlooks the sea, crossed each evening by the illuminated ferryboats *Egnatia* and *Appia*, like two floating castles. Occasionally a stray tourist gets washed ashore and immediately occupies the focal point of curiosity for the villagers, who, when they're not debating the toxic effects of parathion on fruits and vegetables, sit yarning about the wars. A regular patron of the café is the village schoolmaster, who impatiently awaits the evening arrival of the *National Herald*—only newspaper available here—then hides his face in it, while at his side the agriculturalist, bored to death with luxury, begs him for the paper so he can do the crossword. The bourgeois and his wife always dine at the same hour, extolling the island's matchless splendor and enchanting sights. At ten, outside in the darkness, Plutarch lies in wait for the rocket to pass overhead and send him its signal. And all day long his Aunt Elpida carries the water pitcher to and fro on her head, a most picturesque practice for preservationists of pure village customs. Though water is scarce in the village. And electricity, nonexistent.

One day, in a howling northwest gale, the question of why Plutarch didn't want to go to the high school in town was raised. His folks are in a position to send him. The schoolmaster can readily affirm that he's quick to learn, having had him in junior school for three years. I myself, setting him a puzzle to solve—how to make one rectangle and four similar triangles with eight matches—got a quite unexpected solution. He'd made me two rectangles and eight triangles. The bourgeois spouse is inconsolable. "Such a shame," she laments, "clever boys like Plutarch not wanting to study." Yes, objectively it is a shame to let his native wit go to waste. Yet, reluctant to offer him the same facile and unreflecting advice as the others' "go to high school," I ask him, "What d'you want to be?"

"I'm deliberating," he replies, quite serious. "I'm thinking of following my island tradition."

"What tradition?"

"Leave. Be a stewie on a ship, and go to America."

"Stewie," I later learn, means steward, cabin boy. I also learn that most of the island's young men have "skipped to America" by ship. Entered illicitly, that is. Those who gave the immigration officers the slip contrived by arranged marriage to acquire American citizenship. Many have been forced to return empty-handed. Sad stories abound. One lad, having saved hard, gave himself up to the authorities in order to avoid the return fare.

Suddenly the café's packed with them: boys, none above thirty, polite and well-dressed, like tourists in their own village, counting the days before they redepart for their adoptive fatherland, one for San Francisco, another for some obscure little township, the majority for New York. From the way they talk, I soon see that New York is more familiar in the village than Athens. Streets are mentioned, numbers, even by those who've never been. . . . An endless line of fifteen-year-olds appears on the scene, hardly any with an official invitation in his pocket. Most are ready to brave the hazards of "skipping." "After all, what've we got to lose?" they say. "Couple of months in jail, then back." Whereas here in the village it's jail without end. They see the sad plight of their elders assisting bourgeois housewives at their sand baths; running risks with parathion; forever saying last year was better; endless hours incarcerated in the café regurgitating the same old yarns from their army days about mad captains and maniacal majors; sweating for a day's pay, by night left with nothing but a weary day's pain. And they see those back from abroad, no longer just old men come to leave their bones on their native isle but young men, wallets stuffed with dollars, scented cigarettes, lighters that shoot flame to the ceiling, clothes without frays and patches. And inside, within their scarcely molded youthful consciousness, they begin to debate whether the grass might not really be greener. What else can the boy mean when he says he wants to follow his island tradition?

Everyone spouts about the glorious tradition of our race, while the generation bracing up behind us has already evolved a staunch and inglorious tradition of running away. Race becomes an unconditional race to get away, a curious reversal of reality that poses a grave and distressing problem for every conscientious adult seeing a lad like Plutarch not remotely wanting to go to high school. What can you say to him? Go? Then you assume all responsibility for his subsequent misfortunes. Leave? That means the final dissolution, the liquidation of all our animate assets—without due leave of the court of the first instance. It means we've wound up selling demolition materials. Better to follow Puerto Rico's example and emigrate pell-mell to America. But we're not like the Puerto Ricans; we have antiquity, we have the past. Then let a few stay, say five or six, to guard it. To each beacon, a keeper.

Of course, young Plutarch's grandpa, ex-skipper of sail, man of valor capable of nourishing a whole romance full of local color, threatens, half joking, half serious, to take a wet plank and "learn him." But Grandpa's hard of hearing. Of course, the bourgeois pensioner, all the time preoccupied with the picturesqueness of the island, saying go to such and such a rock and you'll see a breathtaking sunset and take such and such a route for the monastery, only be sure to have a stick handy for the dogs—of course, he and his wife are heartbroken that Plutarch doesn't want to go to high school and their Greece, "Greece the Glorious, Greece the Strong" —which today no longer exists—will lose a brilliant scientist, or some such, of tomorrow. But ask the schoolmaster and the agriculturalist, younger, more harassed, and you'll find they've something else to say: "He'd be dumb to go to high school. He'll earn ten times more on the ships or abroad. What did we gain from school? A paltry salary and a slap every time you raise your head."

Suddenly the café's packed with emigrants, with all those forced to create this desperate tradition of flight: coal miners from Belgium, laborers from Germany, dishwashers and restaurateurs from America and Australia, phantoms of men whose thoughts, as the train speeds on into the darkness, veer doggedly rearward like the smoke from a locomotive—among them, many who finished high school. Did this "education" prevent their departure? Did their diploma provide them the prospect of a job? Or did it simply serve to distinguish them in the army from junior-school graduates and those of the superior schools? Given this, unless you're blind or deaf, how can you now advise a bright child to follow the same fate? How, when the child himself can see, beyond the boggy village beach, the open sea? With what credence when this credence has become credit at the grocer's? With what hope when hope is reduced to the name of his aunt? In what spirit when the only spirits haunt the empty motels, the Xenia hotels, the guesthouses of rich monasteries, the dubious funds of ministries, the yachts of shipowners, the ancient theaters where in winter graze the contented cows and docile oxen of the Achaeans? How can you keep from screaming when speech merely adds to the mounting chaos between us and you? At least the inarticulate cry is more universal, because it can be understood even by tourists ignorant of our articulate speech.

Café talk, maybe, but what's wrong with the café when it remains the infallible barometer of our country, the like of which you'll find neither in books, nor in statistics, nor in official sociological surveys? How will you who'll "bear the responsibility if Greece starves," as the occupation posters used to read—you, the anonymous you who already bear such a responsibility—how are you to advise a child to stay in a state that never became a state, which thrived only as a nation scattered across the face of the earth and which from the moment it was hammered into one country inevitably fell into decline? The parallel with the Jews is unavoidable.

Today, in the general bliss of untroubled slumber where the accepted line is "leave the mentally backward alone so they'll vote for us," the enormity of the error no longer fools anyone. Unto us, the evil. Some a little, some a lot, victims of war or victims of peace, according to circumstance we complete the circle. But the generation at our heels, the generation waiting to watch the rocket pass at ten, waiting, wiser and unscarred, to embark on life, will not accept defeat from the outset. Finding no other way out, they'll just skip through the window to another country where work seems to be rewarded; where tacit social distinctions seem to exist but minimally; where not only do the military have all the munitions they need, but doctors all the drugs and teachers all the necessary books; where on café walls they don't serve up such opiates as "Greece is making steady advances. She merits them" and "The sacred tree of Greek liberty is unwithering"; where Canaris doesn't set fire to the flagship of the Turkish fleet under the command of Kapoutan Pasha; where Fatherland—Religion—Family are not the eternal Hellenic principles; where His Majesty isn't forever smiling; where the ship is not forever sinking. . . .

My Village

Two Variations

The village, an extension of the mountain in color and quality of stone, was suffering from necropathy. Gray slates, where tiled roofs would render it independent of the hillside's harshness, resembling workers' peaked caps the same sooty color as the factory walls. The village empty, like a stellar habitation on another planet. The young all obeyed the call to general mobilization; they left, that is, as emigrants to Germany. At one time they used to leave for America, Canada, Australia, Africa. Now only one country attracts them: heavy, industrial, reconstructed Germany, defeated in the war while we, you see, found ourselves on the side of the victors. Even my Aunt Maria, eighty-five years old, her waist girt with a skein of basil, thinks seriously of leaving for Germany. "That's where the shekels are, m'lad. Ain't nothin' here."

The village, drawn like the elastic of a slingshot through the prong of the two mountains, one bald, ashen, all stony, the other, opposite, wooded with those pines not ravaged by the fires, crowned with the ruins of Koufocastro, rests petrified in a final writhe like a harpooned snake with its skin turned scale hard still dipping its head to sup water at the well of Saint Basilica, its tail lost in the vineyards and fig trees that surge forth to greet your coming.

II

No, I have no link with this village with its flat gray tiles like workers' peaked caps, the same color as the factory smokestack. I have no link with this monstrous absence of the young who emigrated en masse to Germany while I stayed, a tourist after so many years, with just my grandma and Aunt Maria for company.

What happened to Lazos the shepherd? What happened to Sotiris, child of the trammel nets? What happened to Mathios and his beehives, boyhood building blocks which he grafted onto the Holy Mount? What happened to Stamatis, with the scar on his arm from the blast of an unexploded mine? What happened to Nikolas, who gathered walnuts and played the flute on Sunday evenings at Poupos' cottage?

No, I have no link with this village laid waste on the harsh mountainside, with the seeds of my hopes that expired in the thighs of the slope, missing the path to the ovaries.

So I remained alone in the room with the ancestral photographs. Grandfathers and grandmothers in an era of ignorance, valiant and virgin, all the oppressive past—all this, to end up in the empty village of my birth squeezed into the ravine, with the Koufocastro, symbol of my desolation. Stellar habitation in an uninhabited region of the moon—all the inhabitants emigrants to the factories of Germany, to Belgian mines.

Here, There's Another God

Crow Mountain and Swallow Mountain face each other. Like Big Village and Little Village perched on their lower slopes. Watching each other like girls from opposite windows. In the intervening gorge, at its deepest point, lies the tiny hamlet of Gavro, which belongs equally to both villages. Two of the lesser heights in the district, the Hide and the Mackerel, are linked by a bridge. Below this bridge runs a stream. Everything about the landscape with its snows and dense firs reminds you of Switzerland. As the sun comes out, the snow-capped peaks shimmer like the domes of Constantinople. . . .

But present tense sounds odd. One dome has collapsed, as at Hagia Sophia, and marred its beauty. Now the Hide is maimed; Little Village, only half-extant, and the bridge vanished under a mountain of rubble. Opposite, the houses of Big Village are left to contemplate the catastrophe their little sister met. . . .

Unprecedented landslide on Swallow Mountain, Evrytania—Little Village is no more—Completely buried—Thirteen dead, many injured— Sixty homes crushed—Seven-day state of emergency proclaimed.

Pictures supplemented the awesome plaguelike image. But the reality is always otherwise. This is how I saw it, that Tuesday morning when I first encountered this spot where, within the space of a few minutes, a whole tragedy had taken place.

It was as if a quarry had suddenly appeared on the belly of the mountain. Or as if one of its cheeks had been torn off and its face left indelibly scared. Discharged rubble, congealed in sooty lava. Plane trees from the ravine bodily uprooted. Sheet iron. Rafters from rooftops. Beams. A rill following the worn course of the stream winds its tortuous way between the mounds of accumulated mud, tinkling mournfully like a dirge for the dead. Unseen cocks accentuate the desolation of the landscape. Mute crows circle seeking carrion. "First they gouge out their eyes, then they rip them to shreds," so the peasant tells me. A donkey haltered amid the debris tosses his head to the right, to the left, in utter incomprehension. Higher, where mountain sundered from mountain, lie heaps of fallen firs like matchsticks spilled from their box, a few still just managing to prop each other up. Now and then in the ravine's vacuous resonance a dry thunderclap rings out—just a falling fir tree. Those homes still left standing to the right of the village patiently await their end. The church bell rings of its own accord, sign that the surface is astir. Next door stands the school, the most "modern" building in the village. I doubt it'll last long. On this intact side, the semicircular terraces descending the slope in steps leave the vanished remainder to your imagination, in the manner of experts reconstructing a fragmented antique pot. The mountain vomit or "cold lava," as they've named it, overlays the ravine and reaches to our very feet as we stand beside the Chapel of the Holy Apostles. It looks like silt deposited by some gigantic bulldozer which you keep expecting to come and unblock the place. Nearby, the Fox Movietone film crew, a huge brand-new American car, more parked vehicles, two minute cops warming themselves around a bonfire—all night they've been on duty guarding the area lest any of the villagers dare venture across—and an itinerant photographer from Lamia taking souvenir snaps, against a background of "biblical catastrophe." The snow falling, sometimes in thick flurries, sometimes in sparse flakes, cloaks with a cold white blanket the freshly dug grave that yawns before us.

I can't help thinking it was one of these fir trees, now fallen, that stood in Syntagma Square for the Christmas festivities, a gift to the capital from the county of Evrytania.

THE VILLAGERS I

The first Little Villagers I met I found in a warm hall inside the Domestic Science College at Karpenission. They'd no relatives to go to so were housed there for the present. They talked to me, still exhausted, panic-stricken. Yet they possessed the calm of the man who's stared death in the face and escaped to tell the tale.

"My name's Athanasios Dougadeles, son of Evangelos. It all happened inside three minutes. I just made it across the bridge. A minute more and I'd have been swallowed alive. I'm a physical wreck. . . . Twenty thousand drachs I had from my wife. Went out day laboring so as not to touch it. Couldn't sleep last night. I was in here and I could hear the wind and I thought now the wave'd come and carry me off for sure. The wave swallowed everything. The avalanche came and covered everything. The world gave a jolt; screams for help went up. Some were gobbled up in the wave, some swept off on top of it."

"My name's Tsinias Pentelis. I was at home with my wife and my daughter, who's four. Gettin' ready to go to church. In the front room when it happened. We tried to get out, but the door was stuck. Then we were carried off, all in one piece. We could see other houses doin' somersaults. We were slidin' along on the wave. House was walkin'. Doors flew off hinges. We just got out in time before the walls collapsed. Streets were gaping. The earth took us down a hundred yards. Threw us up on the highway."

"We didn't even manage to grab a pair of pants," says another. "A cloud of lime came down. Couldn't see a thing. Some just had time to grab a little cash. Us, nothing."

"I'm Christodoulias Georgios, farm laborer. My wife called me first. 'Get up. What are you wating for? The house is all sealed off.' I got out of bed. Made straight for the two trunks to get them out and take them to another house farther down. I thought our house was solid enough to hold firm. 'Aren't you going to take the machine?' says my wife. She's a dressmaker. I went back inside. But the ceiling was coming unstuck and the whole house creaking. *Crrr . . . crrr . . . crrr.* We took off. With a pause here and a pause there we reached dry land where everyone was congregating. My wife has a weak heart. I'd brought some camphor along and we gave her an injection."

The story of Yannis Athanasopoulos, the goatherd buried with his goats, I learn bit by bit from different people. Briefly this is what happened:

Athanasopoulos, aged about thirty, married, two children, herded all the village goats, totaling some 150 head. At that very moment he was just on his way up when someone told him the mountain was caving in. Yannis made straight for the bridge joining the Hide with the Mackerel. The bridge, now buried to a depth of at least 100 feet, stood at a height of some 250 feet above the stream. He was about to cross with his herd when Kouveles' car, coming unsuspectingly from the direction of the village, scattered the goats. The car got across. Yannis delayed a minute, rounding up the goats, conscientiously not wanting to lose even one. But he was too late. That one minute proved fatal. A torrent of earth came hurtling down, struck the rocks on that side of the bridge, then rebounded like a breaker in heavy surf, and swept him off with all his goats. The car, on the other bank, escaped unharmed.

"My name's Christophoros Koutsodemas. I've come up from Athens. That's where I work, in the Seagull Hotel, Varkiza. My sister, thirty days a mother, was Athanasopoulos' wife, the one who perished. I sweated to make her a marriage. I built her the house in Little Village, and together she and her husband built up a little property. Now house, property, and husband are gone. I'm here to take her to Athens because she's had a nervous breakdown. Three times she's tried to do away with herself. The doctor says she needs a change of scene. She's in the hospital now. There's my other sisters, too. And my mother. The whole weight falls on my shoulders. We'll all have to share one room."

With Koutsodemas, his brother-in-law Dermatas, and several others we head for the hospital next door.

His sister, fair like him, so you can't tell how pale she is, is confined to bed, her two children in her arms. She can't speak. Though at one instant I hear her mutter, "I hugged my baby in my arms and tumbled down." The baby, just thirty days old, by a miracle was saved.

In the adjacent beds, their heads bandaged, lie two more women from Little Village. "My name's Constantia Tasou," says a soft-spoken old lady, wife of Georgios Tasou, whose body was the only one to be recovered. "Son, we were picked up in the chaos and swung from bank to bank. 'Don't be afraid,' my husband kept telling me. 'No harm'll come to us.' 'Holy Mother, what curse has befallen us!' I kept saying. We were dropping. It was like tumbling down stairs. Then everything caved in on us. I wound up with just my head stuck out, yelling. Then the fellows from Big Village came and pulled me out. 'You there, Constantia?' 'I'm here. My husband, too.' 'Where is he, Constantia?' 'Here, I tell you; he was holding my leg.' They freed my leg and found his hand. Ah, we lived in Sala eighteen years. We were paupers. We had four girls. We came to Little Village to better ourselves. It was a lusher district. As long as a man lives, he tries to better himself. . . . Ah, why did we ever come?"

Her young neighbor with a bruised face speaks with a strong accent. Her name's Fofo Zographou. "I was in the gorge seeing what I could salvage from my house, when the shutters and iron-work came down on top of me. I was buried up to my waist. I yelled and they all rushed over to pull me out, Dermatas, the priest, Koropes, Zachos, Thodoros, Gabrielides, and Koula's brother Xekarphotos. . . ."

Dermatas takes over; Fofo has difficulty speaking because of the pain from her injuries. "We stuck two beams against the wall to prop it up, then started digging her out. We freed one of her legs, but the other was buried right under the rocks. The wall was swaying, just about to collapse. When we pulled her out we thought she was dead from the waist down. But she'd fallen on top of a caw, so the rocks that flattened her were cushioned from beneath, and no bones were broken. She was right up and walking. The minute we left, the wall gave way."

The tireless Dermatas goes on filling in the details. "Felicity Boura was buried, too, farther down. Someone was yelling, 'A pickax, a pickax to dig out Felicity.' Vassilis Michas was carrying an old lady who was paralyzed. . . . With the earthquake a donkey in the cellar found himself in the kitchen. His master unsaddled him but he was quivering all over. He just stood there haltered. . . . Chickens flying through the air. . . . Let me explain how it happened: the Hide was hollow inside. With the rains that haven't let up for the last three months, the roots of the firs absorbed a lot of water. Thirty years ago a German hydrologist predicted one day Little Village would capsize. From then on his words became legend—"

"My grandma," Fofo interjects, "I remember she used to tell us the proverb, 'Mountain shall merge with mountain.'" As indeed happened.

The Little Village parish priest was in the middle of the "Hymn of the Cherubim" in Holy Mass when all hell let loose. First the schoolmaster and his wife came to tell him all the houses were crumbling. But the priest wouldn't interrupt the mass. Then a chorister's wife came to fetch her husband because their house had started to crack. This chorister perished. The other chorister, who paid no heed to his wife and insisted on not leaving in the middle of mass, was saved. After the blessings, the priest, with all his congregation, sallied forth. Those whose houses were on the other side ran to salvage what they could, with the aid of the rest.

"The people's solidarity and composure," confesses the priest, "were exemplary. Everyone rushed to each other's aid. There were acts of true self-sacrifice. I, together with others, rescued Fofo Zographou, who was buried and screaming, 'Save me, brothers, save me.' The hardest of hearts could not have endured the sight."

"How many were in church at the time of the disaster?"

"Less than usual. About a hundred."

"And the church itself?"

"To all appearances there can be no question of its reofficiation. Inside are vessels of great worth as well as icons from the Holy Mount. It's called Transfiguration of the Saviour and was built with donations from wealthy parishioners and settlers in America. Don't forget that Little Village, though it was burned down by the

Germans and Italians during the occupation, still had two-story houses more luxurious than any you'd find even in Athens. You'd be ashamed to set foot . . ."

In the evening the snow falls thick on Karpenission. Two soldiers, not local boys, stroll into the taverna where we're eating and make for the jukebox. But the landlord points at the unplugged socket.

On the spot were the Minister of Welfare, Mr. Tsatsos, although running a high temperature, Evrytania's High Sheriff, Mr. Tsaousis, E. K. Center Unionist Deputy Mr. Papaspyrou, ERE National Radical Deputy Mr. Karapiperis, the Commissioner of the Constabulary of Central Greece, the Chief Constable of the Evrytania Constabulary, Brigadier Papaconstantinou, Division B Schools Inspector Mr. Katsireas et alii. Queen Frederica has also displayed a lively interest.

On November 10, the village reservoir underwent subsidence. The engineer from the Parish and Borough Technical Service made an immediate estimate of the necessary expenditure for the construction of walls to underprop the reservoir. It didn't occur to a single one of the county's experts that for a reservoir to subside out of the blue there must be something rotten in the village. Nor was anyone perturbed by the fact that a fissure three feet deep had opened a month ago in the overhanging forest. The secretary of Little Village Parish Council refused to comment further. . . . On Thursday one of the villagers saw a crack appearing in the concrete of his back yard. He thought the soil underneath must be soft so decided he'd seal it with cement in a couple of days when he'd be back in the village. "How was I to know the damage was on the inside," he says. Just the other day a delegation of village residents presented themselves at County Hall to report fissures opening in the ground and in their houses. The high sheriff promised to look into the matter forthwith, "but the disaster forestalled us." The villagers' fear of speaking more openly reminds me of Pavlos Kalligas' words written exactly 120 years ago: "The hapless peasants dared not raise their eyes; but bowing their napes bent 'neath the yoke of bondage, held their peace."

Food has been supplied to the victims by the Lamia Military Command. The Metropolitanate has furnished articles of clothing; the American-Canadian organization CARE, writing materials for the schoolchildren. The Greek Red Cross has dispatched clothing and supplies.

Yet I know for a fact that refugees from Little Village housed in the Domestic Science College at Karpenission, slept for two nights on concrete.

THE VILLAGERS II

Those Little Villagers who hadn't gone to Karpenission found shelter in Big Village, with the harrowing sight of their own Paradise Lost constantly before their eyes. Among them, the twelve-year-old son of the Contoyannis family, which sank with almost all hands. The longer the child speaks, the more strongly I sense what it costs him to contain his emotion.

"Me, they sent to the shop"—Contoyannis had the main café in the village square—"to fetch a case to fill up with bits and pieces from the house. My father ran to get to my aunt in time. I saw the house collapse and a great wave sweep them all away. My father, my mother, my sister, and my aunt. My father'd saved 20,000 drachs and was getting ready to leave for Australia in the springtime. That's where my big sister is, the married one. Now there's only us four kids left. My big brother, who's seventeen, me, and the others, eight and five years old."

"My name's Floros Constantinos. I was opposite. Watched the village like at the movies. Matter of a minute. A flash."

"I'm the Big Village constable. The whole thing was instantaneous. One hell of a roar, it all caved in, out shot the rubble, and came down wham! I rescued Constantia Tasou. She was buried up to her neck."

"One time, my boy, there used to be flocks of nightingales here. And tall plane trees in the ravine. In the occupation—you were small and you won't remember—this was Free Greece. Us old'uns with our white beards, we'd sit down in a circle, in the square there, and make all the decisions. The village was burned down by the Germans. But we rebuilt it even prettier. Now this calamity's hit us. Fifteen buried alive. Me so old, and I never saw such a thing in my life. I passed out."

"My name's Panayiotis Matsoukas. I work in Athens. Came to the village to spend Christmas. But I got sick with the flu. My wife says, 'Get up, the village is falling down!' 'Come on, how can a village fall down?' I say. But I got up and went out. Our own house never came down. It's near the church. I went back for my overcoat. The street had capsized, so I cut across the fields to Big Village."

"A threshing floor, and three cows dropped a couple of hundred feet, and the cows weren't scratched."

AT GAVRO

Gavro, in the gorge, has hardly any dwellings. It's always served as a relay between the outlying villages of Evrytania and the town of Karpenission. Those going there on business would spend the night in this hamlet, which besides the two face-to-face cafés can also boast a big emigration agency, "The Beacon—for America, Australia, Canada," right next to a wall emblazoned with three huge blue letters: ERE.

Since this morning—the third after the avalanche—the villagers have been getting ready to go back to Little Village to salvage whatever they can from the few houses left standing. Though the streets have capsized and it's impossible to cross the quagmire in the fields with laden beasts, they've brought several mules with them just in case.

But on arrival at Gavro, they learned it's prohibited to go near their village "until further notice." Also, the chief constable is there, keeping watch to see no one slips across on the sly. Outside, the blizzard rages, and the Little Villagers crowd into the two cafés, mute, pensive, listening to a cabdriver from Lamia and a visitor from the outlying villages saying there's bright sunshine everywhere. "Here, there's another God." Get to their village or not, they certainly don't seem about to budge. This is their patch, and here they'll stay despite all danger. The whole atmosphere conjures up a prerevolutionary Russian railway station with the muzhiks waiting in the snow for their train. However late the train, they wait on, uncomplaining.

Experts are already at work on the problem of resettlement. First and foremost a suitable site must of course be sought. Geologists have already begun research to this end, and favor the view that resettlement cannot of necessity be implemented here.

Alack if it can't! Not a man among them will go to a place he doesn't know. Here they've lived; here they want to live. Close to their dead loved ones they can never disinter. Close to their scuttled homes. Their silence and their seeming composure—they haven't yet recovered from the shock—mask a profound obstinacy. Their tie with this earth is stronger than the ties of blood. Watching them shuffle from one café to the other, their sole estate the few tattered clothes on their backs, I reflect how with the coming years that black Sunday will pass into legend. They'll talk of the earth that turned into a torrent, of the wave that drowned them. Old men who recollect the catastrophe of their childhood will tell their grandchildren, "Here, once. Alas, only for those entombed alive, as in a Belgian coal mine!"

From the Xenia tourist hotel journalists dispatch their reports. A lady is worried about the flow of tourists to the area. She's afraid with this landslide it may drastically slump. What's bitten all the newspapers to make them write so much? Did they ever write a word when this was paradise? A man talks of the panic that seized neighboring villages perched like eyries on mountain peaks. The tiniest crack in the wall terrifies everyone. Officials come and go in and out of the hotel. Now the brigadier, now the high sheriff, now some inspector. They go to the toilet, they wash their hands. The girls fix coffee. Chimneys billow from burning stoves. In church the priest prays that the souls may rest in peace. And the snow keeps falling. Falling on Karpenission, on the Swallow and on the Crow, falling on the rooftops, on the bell towers, on the trees. Falling, too, on the few houses still standing in Little Village, on the fields and on the beasts. Falling faintly on the black capes of the herdsmen, on the windows of the cars. Faintly falling, like the descent of their last end, upon all the living and the dead.

The Conversion of the Mussulmans

I was born in Kavala and as a small boy enjoyed her happy pre-war years. The days when the big tobacco merchants would burn a thousand-drachma bill to light a cigar, have ships illuminated to enhance the view from their verandas at the parties they gave. The days when the phrase "my daughter's marrying a tobacco worker" meant something because his trade was safeguarded and he took home virtually a director's salary. In those days the tobacco growers lived well; they sold tobacco at a pound per oka and each year brought wider cultivation. The village of Paradise, beside the river Nestos, was indeed paradise. In those days mildew hadn't yet made its appearance in the villages.

The day war was declared I was standing with my schoolbag on the crest of the hill at Saint John's. The bells were ringing, and the harbor below shimmered festively. I caught sight of Mrs. Patra scurrying in slippers, curlers, and bathrobe down the steps that led to our house. "What is it?" I asked. "War," she replied. Since I had no idea what war meant, I was all ears as she pointed toward the mountain facing us and added, "There! That's where the Bulgars'll come from!"

In fact, one day the Bulgars did come, though I can't say if it was from that mountain or from Saint Silas; and we set off as a refugee family for Salonika. The river Strymon marked the border between the two occupied zones. To get beyond the Bulgarian guardhouse and enter the German occupied zone on the other side of the river, we had to wait our turn in the bus behind an interminable procession of carts and vehicles passing the checkpoint. We were so far from the checkpoint we couldn't even see the Amphipolis Lion. We'd probably have waited a day or two if my mother, who'd fixed some doughnuts for the journey, hadn't used them to cajole a Bulgarian officer, who afterward admitted he was a music lover, too. A piano player herself, my mother engaged him in a conversational duet on Chopin, thanks to which we were allowed through first.

Throughout the occupation, my grandpa kept sending us Bulgarian caramels from Kavala.

After the liberation we returned, because my father was a staunch believer in repatriation. I resumed attendance at junior school and then went on to Karyotakis High, but now life was different in Kavala. We were hungry.

Kavala's port permanently harbors a flotilla of mine sweepers to fish mines out of the northern Aegean between Athos, Thasos, and Samothrace. One such mine exploded once off a Thasos headland where I was fishing with my cousin Stamatis. The mistral's breakers washed it up, detached from the deep, like a sea bloom. The place was suddenly full of giddy fish, swept out to sea on the strong currents toward the Holy Mount.

In 1947, we returned to Salonika. This time we crossed the Strymon by raft, the bridge having been blown up. Each time we crossed, we'd see snarled-up corpses of the rebel resistance on its banks.

We came back to Kavala only in the summertime, on the eve of Prophet Elias' Day, which my grandpa celebrated while my grandma made her own ice cream. This ice cream and the hot bath I'd have in our patrimonial home—the heater was a wood burner—were the only things that still tied me to the town where I was born.

Kavala today, fifty years after her liberation from the Turks, is in a much worse state than before the war, with yet darker prospects for the future. On account of tobacco, the city's sole resource.

In 1953, the Tobacco Employment Act amalgamated TAF— Tobacco Workers' Assurance Fund—with IKA, the Social Security plan. Special tickets were abolished. The tobacco worker's trade is now without safeguards. The new statute is explicit from its very first article. "Those heretofore possessed of such special tickets are henceforth deprived of their right of employment in the processing of the tobacco leaf." Hence the immediate exodus of thousands of people from their closed shop, with a lump sum or as pensioners, while for those just entering, the new statute concedes all rights to the employers. Article 9, paragraph 4: "Those hired for the processing of tobacco are regarded as hired by contract of fixed duration—six days, from Monday until Saturday—expiring ipso jure every Saturday, irrespective of whether the day of engagement be subsequent to Monday. . . ." The tobacco worker is no longer in a position to know if he'll have a job next week, nor can his female counterpart, if she doesn't suit the boss's whim or behave with the overseer, be sure of staying on. Today, this uninspected hiring of labor in the tobacco-curing sheds is based exclusively on pull, on whom you know, on the employers' fancy, on the inscrutable axiom, "You'll do. You won't do."

This first wound in the body of tobacco workers was soon deepened by the introduction of semiautomation to the processing of tobacco, with full automation in view. The admission of the machine to the traditional method of processing by hand laid off thousands of workers, at the same time shortening the job's duration. In concrete terms, where a firm producing 1 million okas of tobacco per year used to keep 1,000 workers busy plucking for 200 working days each, today, with the mechanical plucker, the same quantity of tobacco requires only 250 workers for 80 working days. Where before 70 to 80 treaders were needed, the semiautomated system makes 12 to 14 sufficient, while full automation requires just 2 press operators.

It's natural for every businessman to aim for greater profit. But what about the tobacco workers, those who labor for their daily bread? Thirty to forty drachmas clear is a woman's daily wage, sixty-two to sixty-three, the daily wage of a tobacco worker, stacker or treader. And the work is seasonal—three to four months a year for women and five to six for men. The rest of the time they're unemployed. And things are going from bad to worse as working conditions inside the sheds gradually deteriorate. Present-day sheds are little more than sweatshops. Where before the war a female plucker, a woman who separates the tobacco leaves, was required to produce six to seven okas a day, nowadays she's required to produce twenty-five kilos! Otherwise, on Saturday, fired. Many of the women faint. No first aid. The least hint of chatter during working hours is forbidden. Whip-cracking taskmasters prowl the floor. Who dares speak? No safeguards in this trade. Outside the curing shed wait lines of the jobless.

To those worthies who've busied themselves for years with the problems of the tobacco industry, there seems nothing for it but to nationalize. Yet the present ills have deeper roots. Three companies purchase the greater part of our "classic" tobaccos: American Tobacco, Glen Tobacco, and the German firm Raetz. Each year these foreign trusts fix the prices of tobacco, the East follows suit. Through their underlings—two or three big local tobacco dealers, who act as their executive agents—they make themselves masters of our fate. For Kavala's fate is bound up with tobacco, interwoven with its processing. And foreigners are imposing the new processing systems, setting up in Salonika and expanding outward with the object of eliminating Kavala entirely from the place of cultivation and lading the tobacco direct from field to steamboat; so it's clear what's in store. The government allies itself with these foreigners and, instead of aiding small tobacco merchants who presently conduct a more orthodox commerce, is leading them to the slaughter. Capital is thus gradually concentrating itself in certain hands, hands that will have the entire area at their mercy.

This year the tobacco villages discharged their debts. Mildew infected the neighboring lands. But the city of Kavala remains an open wound from which flows all her blood, out and away. Last year 3,000 souls emigrated from this city alone. . . .

Civilization is Cleanliness: For your medical examination by the Ger-

man Commission it is *absolutely essential* that you present yourself
spotless, clean-shaven, feet washed and shoes polished.

—Printed announcement from the emigration bureaus

This year, after so long an absence, I went back to see the house
where I was born, at Potamoudia. I ran into a friend of ours, an
old lady named Eriphyle. She led me to her "house," one of the
"squat shacks," hand-built by the destitute in the old Vix reservoirs,
where, under the Turks, cisterns collected water and supplied the
town below. In this ravine, against its flanks, at night in the rain,
Eriphyle had built a shelter, just as others had done. Then one
day someone talked, and the authorities arrived with their tape
measures. The police brought charges, they were fined 500 drachmas apiece, and now they're lying low up there, just under the
sanatorium. From the highest of the "squat shacks" you can see
Pentacossia, Souyelo, Saint Athanasios, Youftika, Saint Nikolas,
Fourio, the Virgin, the Arches, Saint Paul, and the Chapel of the
Prophet Elias.

First Eriphyle began wailing her grievances; then gradually the
other women of the settlement gathered round. All jobless tobacco
workers. And all with a single grievance.

"They want young ones in the sheds. The ones they fancy. They
don't want us old folks."

"Work we need. Give us stone, we'll squeeze blood out of it."

" 'You're old and wrinkled,' they say. 'You're past it.' "

"Down at the Labor Center they wouldn't register us. They
threw us out in the street."

"We have no tickets and no jobs. All night we wait outside the
sheds. If you don't know the overseer, the boss, they won't take
you on."

"All for this hovel, I've grown old. They wanted to pull it down.
I half killed myself, I yelled at the cop—"

"In the winter we had no wood to burn. Lucky the forestry's
just above. They gave us some."

"They won't give me a job because my husband's on disablement pension."

"Last year I managed fifty-four working days, but there was a lot more weeping than working."

"We get by on 600 drachs, four of us."

"My son's a soldier and I haven't even a hundred drachs to send him."

"We're not Communists; we're not anything. It's work we want, and bread to eat."

"Those who do work, they're so worn out they can't sleep nights. Like machines they want 'em to work, with their bare hands. We're just longing for a job to do. Too bad if they work us to the bone."

"Me, I don't know what to say. If my husband was here—he works on the fishing boats—he could tell you."

"The other day one of the women came to my place for a fitting. The poor wretch was in tears. She was packing and they put her on plucking. 'You see,' she kept saying, 'come Saturday they'll fire me. I manage eighteen kilos of tobacco. They want twenty-five.' "

"There's a lot goes on between the bosses and the women workers. First it's the overseer, then the foreman, and they end up in the director's car. That's a fact I'm telling you, not just idle gossip."

"So why shouldn't we ask to go to Germany? But even for that you need pull."

In the countries of the Free World the workers, with the strength vouchsafed them by their own merit, have boosted their standard of living. In the Iron Curtain countries, where the horror of red fascism is rife, the workers have been reduced to an amorphous herd of beasts of burden. . . .

—Billposters of the nationalist organization Azure Phalanx

The inspector of labor coolly slurps his melted ice cream. A mother enters his office by the side door and asks him to find her a place in some curing shed.

"Just bide your time."

"How long, son?"

"What can I do?"

"God bless you, I don't have a penny to my name. . . ."

"Come back tomorrow."

A young man comes in and reports that he was hired at one of the sheds as a treader but they're using him as a stacker.

"Have the case looked into," the inspector tells his subordinate, coldly, cerebrally. Then, turning to me, "Daily I go through this charade. There's only one solution—a crusade for the conversion of the Mussulmans."

Suddenly, mounting the rise toward my grandpa's house, next to the Koufler villa, where I used to hunt sparrows with my slingshot, I see the tennis club, now overgrown with grass, terraces dilapidated, and clubhouse closed. A goat undisturbed on what used to be the tennis court. I recall that once, when I was a ball boy, a ball spun off and clouted the wife of a tobacco merchant quite hard. All her facepowder shook off, blanching the gin rummy cards before her. I recall her face, close up, as I went to retrieve the ball, without make-up, like a skull or an African mask. So the tennis club's closed, I muse now. The tobacco merchants avoid appearing in public, in exposed places, so as not to rouse the indignation of the masses. A closed caste, like the shipowners, living an exclusive life as far from Kavala as they can. They might at least have left a little money in the place where they made it! Only one has built a mansion. The others squander their gains elsewhere. I don't speak in anger. The figures say it for me: the annual income of 12,000 tobacco workers is equal to the annual income of twelve tobacco merchants.

Descending later, I encounter those drab streets where, in the old days after six when the sheds knocked off, you couldn't get by, so dense was the wave of tobacco workers heading for the slums. A swarm of bees with no queen. Now not only has the machine taken their place, but the law allows each shed to operate whenever and whatever hours it wishes. During the curing season, it may even work the whole twenty-four, in shifts. The municipal street sprinkler grinds past, drenching the blistering flagstones. Moskov Curing Shed, Commercial, Papastratou, Misirian, Krandonelli, Theodoridi, Austro-Hellenic, EOK, Ataktidi, Pielloglou, Jordanoglou, Petridi . . . The smell of unripe tobacco trusses exudes, pungent, from their barred windows, where countless swastikas recall the Nazi *Vorarbeit*.

As night falls, the new sea front, still not completed—rubble's been laid but not leveled—gradually fills with people come for a stroll by the motionless caïques. Once, before the embankment, the evening stroll took place in the bride bazaar on Omonia Street, Kavala's main thoroughfare, all shopwindows, stores, and patisseries. The stroll always started from the Fessa bakery and ended at the county court. Up and down, down and up, and beyond this street darkness, desolation, and mute tobacco warehouses. Now the sea has opened a new window. At the far end the NOK—Kavala's nautical club—tourist pavilion glows white with its lights. Right opposite, the Beauteous Mytilene restaurant boasts fresh seafoods.

On Fouat Square, site of the vaulted tomb of the mother of Mohammed Ali, founder of the Egyptian dynasty, the municipal band is playing. A meandering Karyotakian ambience, beneath three mammoth advertisements wounding the full-moon sky, saturates me. Yonder, selling like hot cakes, the Athens afternoon papers, the capital's sole contact with its provinces, pre-election period and theatrical tours excepted.

By night, in moonlight, with her poverty and the tumid bulks of the tobacco warehouses expunged, Kavala transforms into a truly magical city. Her amphitheatrical setting, the ample embrace of her bay, never monotonous like the bay of Salonika, especially viewed from the beacon from which you can see both curves, sustains a charm of its own. The hand of Mohammed Ali, mounted on his steed before the house where he was born, points north, a course which, alas, many have been forced to follow.

The following day. In a nook wedged between the warehouse blocks, the workers are snatching a quick bite to eat.

"The life's being sucked from us," says a beardless dock worker. "We ought to go elsewhere. It's the galleys. Fifty-one and a half drachs a day. You can't even eat on that. And you need shoes, don't you? You need a cup of coffee. In wartime I worked in Germany. The Bulgars were here; life wasn't worth living. So as not to wind up hostages, we went over there as workers. A double-trouble job, in Sneinbern, Libinaun. Filling bombs with dynamite. Fire in our hands and fire overhead with the blitz, but we were happier. Franz the Austrian used to say to us, 'What'll you do when the war's over?' And we'd tell him, 'Go back where we belong.' We came back. But over there we were more contented. Now I can't go back. I'm overage. But if I did I'd drag every Greek along with me. . . . My name's Leonidas Markopoulos. Write it down. Write my only joy would be to go back to Germany. . . ."

Some tobacco workers are eating at the next table. I question them.

"Eight hours a day humping trusses up and down a hundred steps to and from the press. Every two hours only can we roll a smoke."

" '*Islé yovan islé, tsiflik senin,*' says a Turkish proverb." "Meaning," explains another, " 'if you work hard, one day the farm'll be yours.' So we work hard. . . ."

"*Kismetlen olmaz,*" adds a third with a sigh. " 'Born poor, die poor.' "

"Up on the mountain," says the first, "you'll see a great big cross. There ought to be a lot more. Specially wintertime, Kavala turns into a graveyard."

"How many months d'you work?"

"We stackers, five or six. We start work as soon as the tobacco arrives from the villages. The other skills work only three or four."

"And the rest of the time?"

"We're idle. We look for work. If you've completed a certain number of days' work, you're entitled to two months' unemployment benefit at 950 drachs a month. And 1,030 if you have two kids."

"The laws were made so only they'd have rights. We have no rights at all. You'd think they were the only Greeks."

"Conditions in the sheds are worse than Dachau."

"I worked eight years for the State Tobacco Organization. They laid me off with not a penny compensation. We're not entitled to compensation, they say, because it's a seasonal occupation."

"And your union?"

"The Stackers' Union does nothing. Or the Labor Center either. They've all sold out."

"Twenty-five hundred of us men and 5,000 women, and for eight months of the year we can just go whistle. . . ."

"Redundancy here isn't quite what you suppose," a retired army officer settled comfortably in a responsible semiofficial post says. "But they've all learned to fold their arms and say, 'Give us a dime.' Eighty per cent of the unemployed are idlers and twenty per cent mentally deficient."

If I didn't know that these are the precise ratios allowable by the army in several of its superior cadres, I just might've misconstrued. . . .

Every afternoon at quarter past one the Pullman boats set sail from the harbor for Thasos, the *Alexis* bound for Limena, the *Maria* and the *Papageorgiou* bound for Limenaria-Poto, as well as two car ferries operating between Keramoti and Limena. In recent years Thasos has undergone a one-sided boost in tourism. Though ringed with beaches, with pines descending like sheep to graze at the cool sea's edge, the whole burden of tourist concern has been thrown around Limena, so that, were the island a big ship, she'd list to that side and sink.

Today, after fifty-one years of freedom, Thasos, like most of the islands, is scourged by unemployment, poverty, and their natural outcome, emigration. Of the total 300 young people living in my father's village, Theologo, 298 have gone. Only my cousin stayed behind selling on credit—cash is a rare commodity in the village— with one other engaged in council affairs. Recently seventy women from another main village had all their papers in order to leave. On the eve of departure their husbands gave them such a thrashing not one of them got away. Stories abound among the locals about émigrés who've remarried without a divorce, without even informing their legal spouse. One wife set out to find her husband in Germany, having heard he'd got married in a registry office over there. His German wife opened the door. "Here, he's mine," she told her. "In Greece, he's yours." On the boat now there are two girls back from Belgium sporting pants and transistors, bound for their village, Mariès.

At the Mariès wharf the rocks are ashen from the ore they used to lade the ships with. Two half-submerged barges testify to long disuse. The Chondrodemos mines, sole industry for the islanders after work in tobacco gave out, have months since extinguished their furnaces. The company ran aground when it tried to compete with Krupp's mining company based on Limenaria. Chondrodemos still owes money to the workers. Meanwhile Thasites go hungry. They live off their olives, and if there's not a good crop this year, winter bodes ill. The beehives and timber and fish are not adequate. After fifty-one years of freedom, Thasos, without a hospital or a high school, and with 15,000 souls awaiting rain like manna, is slowly being expropriated by foreign capital come to infest her beautiful beaches with villas and bungalows.

"The Sphinx Spake." "Grand Display by Barefoot Fire Walkers. Sunday, 17 June. Municipal Stadium." "Thermal Baths: The Orient." "Federation of Taxidrivers: Solidarity."

Ascending again, to look up my godmother, Evlalia, pondering, I ask myself how it happened that there in the center of the city that eight-story monstrosity sprouted five floors higher than the tobacco warehouses, like the tumid bulk of some undercover organization, while other buildings—the Social Security, the Officers' Club, the museum nearing completion and destined to house all the region's finds, from gilt trinkets to Abderan terra cottas—respect the amphitheatrical gradations and horseshoe shape of Kavala with their plane architecture. Despite the lack of industry, there does exist a limited industrial belt, like the woker's belt measuring the girth of his hunger. So let the rich go build their mausoleums there and not in the heart of the city.

My godmother now lives in the Imaret, gift from Mohammed Ali to his birthplace. The Imaret, "namely a seminary with board equipped for over 150 Turkish theological students," is today a hive of the destitute. In its cells that reek from the communal latrines live whole families paying fifty to a hundred drachmas in rent. "And they don't always pay," the warden tells me. "But what can you do with them? Evict? Lawyers have to be paid. Put them in jail? The state has to pay ten drachs a day maintenance. So we leave them be. And the Imaret's falling apart. Minister des Wakouf of the Egyptian government, who owns it, sends us just 500 pounds a year subsidy. Should we spend the money on maintenance or to pay ourselves, the five attendants? Because we have Mohammed Ali's house to attend to and the burial gardens of his parents besides. Before Nasser came on the scene, the bey used to send us 3,500 pounds subsidy. Things were fine then."

In this magnificent edifice, with its silvered cupolas and ornamental Coptic script, live sick bodies and wounded beasts, as in a rare seashell. Evlalia shows me into her cell, with its single fanlight. Her husband's away fishing. Drain water in the courtyards, and more cats than rats. Human misery once more, in its most tragic concentration, confutes, the minute I emerge, all the beauty of the harbor, all the picturesqueness of the locale, all the progress seemingly achieved with the laying of the new underground telephone cables. I doubt if today in the dungeons of Egypt one would find such inhuman squalor as one encounters in the "wakoufs" of Mohammed Ali in Kavala.

Taking a last stroll around the city, I note the new state hospital, near the Karnagio naval dockyard, and I rejoice. I note the renovation of the judicial chambers and I rejoice. The new civic buses. I even rejoice over the new urinals erected beside the overgrown arches. I rejoice for the garden city, for the fishing berth which is to become the "regular anchorage for fishing vessels," by the mill. . . .

Climbing the hill to see my grandpa, who saved the mill from being blown up during the Bulgarian occupation, I find the yard where I played as a small boy before the war, when it had the dimensions of a whole world. Now there's barely room for me. The neighborhood where I heard the chimes of war. . . . The harbor shimmering below. . . . And my grandpa, who sees little and hears less, starts yarning about the liberation of Kavala and the conversion of the Mussulmans. . . .

Two

Salonika: The New Theater

"And our city?" I asked him, to change the subject.
"Just as you left it."
"Is the theater built, next to the Macedonian Society?"
"No. It's still being built. . . ."

—*The Angel*

When I graduated from the Academy of Auxiliary Angels of the Heavens—AAAH—in the gilt full dress of an angel cadet and proud of my plastic wings, I arrived, on a few days' leave from the monastic star where we trained, in my city, Salonika. Even before landing, on my long descent through denser and dénser strata of polluted air, I was surprised and shocked to see, beside the White Tower, the marble-wrought edifice of the theater now complete. I couldn't believe my eyes because—and this is hard to understand unless you have lived through the fifties in Salonika —for ten whole years we watched it being built with still no sign of completion. In those days it came to be the anguish of our youth. Hence my dismay on seeing it from on high almost finished. I say almost, because, losing altitude, I spotted some scaffolding which roused my anxiety. After dropping by at home and spending a little time with my folks, I left my wings in the suitcase and hurried off to admire it. Now I stood gazing at it, not daring to tell myself I wasn't pleased. Perhaps with my absence for years from earth I'd grown unused to things human. I therefore thought it more proper to ask the opinion of others, informed or otherwise. So here goes, like the game consequences we used to play as kids on the sands of Thasos. "How d'you do. I've been hearing a lot about you, good and not so good. Now listen . . ."

A university professor told me, "Salonika has quite the richest tradition of Byzantine architecture. From the simple early Christian basilicas down to the elegant creations of the final years of the empire stretches an unbroken line of majestic monuments. This is followed by the popular architecture of the Turkish domination and finally a number of neoclassical buildings like the Central Administration and the university, which, while unpretentious, supply with their noble and decorous form a tone of antique distinction. To this heritage we came and added countless obnoxious apartment blocks and several quite anomalous buildings.

"This theater might have been one more such maladroit erection, were it not above all boorish, with its howling pretensions to glamour, its air of nouveaux riches flaunting their gaudy baubles and glamourous finery. It stands outside time and place, far removed from the authentic Greek tradition of simplicity inspired with genius."

An architect told me, "Stylistically the theater building subscribes to no recognizable style. It's neither modern, as it might have been, nor classical, nor baroque, nor neoclassical. Even taking it as 'original,' as the personal inspiration of its creator, we're bound to acknowledge errors aplenty. First, the colonnade of the convex section, in form and extent, in relation to the projections on either side and to the remainder of the section, is quite untenable. Secondly, a structure on the roof, like an apartment-block recess, seems totally irrelevant. Thirdly, the two transverse sections form successive piers which chromatically and in their relative proportions are incongruous. Fourth, the Officers' Club and the theater clash, cerebrally speaking. On the one hand, the club tends to submit to the perceptual curve of the White Tower, while, on the other, the theater tends to negate it. And last but not least, the amorphous wedge between the old Society of Macedonian Studies and the theater, at present a garage and supposedly to become an arcade joining the two buildings, does not solve our problem but merely augments it. . . ." He seemed bent on analyzing one by one all the theater's defects, but for the forceful interventions of a second architect.

"Why confuse the lad with so many superfluous details?" As I was about to protest, he resumed. "The sad truth is, not one Greek town is built to an over-all design, to what the Americans call a master plan. Which has stunted Salonika's proper development. While the visitor gets the impression of a Central European megalopolis with copious thoroughfares and commodious inter-communicating junctions, at many points, particularly up in the Old Town, the new apartment buildings have reduced her to a kind of Neapolitan clothesline. To me, the theater's less of a tragedy than it is to see an eight-story apartment house built on the site of a two-story house with no proportional widening of the street. You know, abroad they preserve every house of any historical merit. Salonika has plenty. But what happens? They pull them all down, so destroying all sense of history. Soon we won't know where we are. The Byzantine parts won't suffice to persuade us we're in Byzantium's second city. In this climate of wholesale destruction you can see what I mean about the theater. One basic fault I find is that people expect lessons in optics from public buildings. When public buildings are bad, public taste is bound to suffer. While the museum breathes peacefully in the airy space of the fair, the theater's vulgarity murders the square and distorts the scale of the White Tower. Because whichever way you look at it the theater has *everything*. Marble, aluminum, projec-tions, recesses, colors, plaster, wooden constructs, big windows, small windows, velvet, plastic. Variety can be aesthetically useful, but it's not always indispensable. Marble and plaster are inter-spersed for no good reason. As a building, it can be traced to the architectural spirit prevalent around 1901, and to that spirit's least meritorious vein. . . ."

I stepped out on the street, profoundly dismayed and distressed with what I'd heard from the experts. On my way to take a look inside, I stopped a couple of passers-by. "It's like the tomb of the Pharaohs," said one. And the other, possibly a composer, "It's like Elgar's 'Pomp and Circumstance.'" Then I stepped inside.

Marble, white, black, and gray mottled, greeted the feel of my footsteps. A low ceiling lit by almond clusters. *Pull-pull-pull*. Walls with coffee-colored-marble décor, all dainty flutings and filigree,

weighing you down, making you want to stoop. Stairs. Four octa-
gonal pillars decked with marble, and herringbone marble under-
foot. Above, a sort of gallery or foyer. The section to the right
painted vivid orange like a virgin's bedroom. To the left an insipid
cherry like an old maid's bedchamber. *Push-push-push*. Circular
ashtrays at the base of the pillars. A handful of sand for a candle
to my grandma's memory. A chill in the air. Stairways leading to
further marbled levels. Bathroom appliances on the walls, here the
color of instant-coffee dregs. Marble gunnels to the side of the
stairs that as a kid I'd have slid down. A motionless centipede of
frosted lights on the ceiling. Mounting these stairs to the second
floor—the first is to house the future cinema—you find yourself
facing an empty space where large vermilion-colored squares, the
first not of marble, greet you like vacancies for statues, for busts
of the builders. Upward of this gallery your eyes behold a cataract
of marble fashioned into twenty-one narrow, outward-bellying
stairs leading to a narrow door like the twin doors in the stage
set for ancient tragedies. Therein, you imagine, the murders and
the incest will be enacted and the actors will emerge on the platform above to declaim the horrors. Yet, no. Mount these stairs
and you find yourself, via the narrow doorway, in the orchestra
of the theater. Red velvet, as on the padded doors, swathes the
soft seats, a red curtain screens the stage, and red, again, drapes
the balconies. The seats hold you bolt upright, as if sleep is strictly
prohibited.

Making my exit from the pit and my ascent toward the boxes
and the two galleries, I notice the stairs narrowing, the gleam on
the marble fading, the colors altering in inexhaustible variety, the
floor fitted with blue plastic and the ceiling lights with the look
of landing boats. Descending by the same route, trying not to sully
the marble being polished by a whole platoon of middle-aged
charwomen, I feel as if I'm somewhere behind the great Mauso-
leum at Forest Lawn Cemetery, where the dead lie in drawers of
marble, where marble likewise predominates to intensify the chill
of death. The feeling of a monster snail—were it but an architec-

tural snail like the Guggenheim Museum in New York—concealing within its huge protective shell a morsel of food. Such, in relation to the surrounding space, is the actual theater. "On the theater's various levels space must be contrived for the provision of ladies' and gentlemen's toilets. . . ." Such toilets there are in abundance. "The stairways must be duly situated to render evacuation at all points convenient and speedy. . . ." Such is more than the case. But what about the charter's provision, "if for aesthetic reasons this is deemed necessary"?

"Anyway, the King liked it," the commissionaire informed me down in the lobby, seeing me somewhat soured.

"Which King?" I inquired. "His Marble Majesty, maybe?"

My barber was overjoyed to see me after so long. "What d'you think of the theater building?" I asked him.

"A true rarity," he said. "Everyone's in raptures about it. A lot of money's been spent, and will be. . . . A true masterpiece."

"Have you been inside?"

"Apparently . . . we hear from the critics. They can't find words to describe it."

"Doesn't it blot out the White Tower?"

"The tower's been blotted out for years. . . . Ten years ago, when we used to go up to Forty Churches, the topnotch residential area—mark that, topnotch—we could see every inch of the White Tower, even down to the photographers at the bottom. Now you can just see the flagstaff."

"That's better, is it?"

"Much better."

"To my mind," I said as he was clipping my sideburns, "the White Tower, as symbol of Salonika, ought to stand out clearly."

"But it does stand out, my old boy. When you come in on the steamboat, the White Tower and the theater and the park and the photographers—it all stands out."

During my few days in Salonika I asked many other people for their opinion of the new theater. A breviary of their replies follows.

A university lecturer in line for a professorship: "It could be better, but as it is it's all right. It's an acquisition for Salonika. Despite not being quite in the modern class, being somewhat ponderous as a building, it does impress favorably. The outer marblework might've been more Hellenic in color. Though the acoustics are superb, I might've had some reservations about the colors inside, which form neither contrast nor composition. . . ."

An interior decorator: "Rather decomposition, because their atonality doesn't allow us to form a clear notion of the space in which we find ourselves. It may be a painter's solution, but it's not architectural. White's perhaps the one color on which the shadow of any foreign object creates semitones. With red the same doesn't apply. I'm against imperial solutions by imperial means."

A philosopher: "I think any polemic on the theater is out of date. Nothing ever happens in this place. When something finally does, everybody takes the opportunity to knock it. One must stress the patience of Mr. Letsas in managing with his walking stick to drum up so much money. In any case, the building, viewed philosophically, is hideous."

A restaurateur: "It's heavy, like moussaka."

A passer-by: "Is it finished?"

Curious to see and learn what the management of the State Theater thought, housed there since October 26 (the day of the official inauguration, in the presence of royalty, government, et cetera, for the fiftieth anniversary of the liberation of Salonika), I entered once more, this time by the side door, which I opened to find myself in a rambling barnlike enclosure. Girders, lime, putty, stone, all hodgepodge like novels by Pentzikis, but lacking their total transcendence to a higher order. To reach the heights I had to use a ramshackle elevator which the super assured me, to boost my courage, breaks down only three times a day and today had already filled its quota. I emerged in a half-finished apartment-house corridor. In a room with a single fanlight the director of the State Theater seemed suddenly like a prison warden. Desks, telephones, typewriters, typists, papers, people, armchairs, all present to an equal degree.

"We're still a little disorganized," the director said courteously, "but we hope soon to . . ."

A law student: "Premeditated bulk, premeditated variety, unpremeditated failure."

An attorney: "A display of prosperity which in the opinion of Premier Karamanlis is superior to that of Scandinavia."

Two basketball players: "It's great. As we've no great buildings in our city, this'll do fine. Whichever way you look at it, it's no monstrosity. Sure . . ."

Another attorney: "Its perpetrator is a felon commissioned in the name of the public."

A spectator in the second balcony: "In the auditorium you can hear well enough but see little. Up top I saw only half the play. My brother-in-law, in the orchestra, saw the other half. Afterward we sat down and filled each other in. . . . Next time I'm going to demand a seat with a view."

A society lady: "Some Athenians have already knocked it, out of envy. . . . Salonika needed it."

A workman: "Inside you need a guidebook just to keep your bearings."

A seamstress: "It lacks simplicity and economy. Pleats are no longer in vogue."

A poet of inner space: "It's like Kazantzakis' *Odyssey*."

An electrician: "It blocks the view of the park."

A professor of English: "Seen from the park it looks like a tobacco-curing shed."

A trade-unionist: "The Bolshoi of the Macedonian capital."

A Greek-American lady: "Something built by Greeks from the States."

A person: "It's like an oilstove to warm the city when the Vardar blows from the north."

A clerk and amateur angler: "The theater's a monster cast up by the sea at the foot of the White Tower. A swollen carcass with its ribs oozing bile and clotted blood leaving marble scabs all over."

Maybe I could've got more, good and not so good, but my leave was up. I unpacked my wings from the suitcase and, leaving this city which I so loved, set out to present myself to the angel battalion to which I'd been posted, yonder, near the frontier of the Hellenic heavens.

Salonika: The Last Day of the Occupation

It was like a Sunday. Shops all shut and streets deserted. From the balcony of our apartment on the fourth floor, corner of Hermes and Aristotle, I could see a fraction of the sun-bathed sea, a section of the zigzag of the mole, while the real harbor where the big ships unloaded their cargo remained invisible. Everything stood stock-still in the undermined silence, ignorant of its impending doom.

Five to twelve: my anguish has reached its peak. At twelve the harbor's to be blown up. The departing Germans have no intention of leaving it intact to the Allies. Though the Allies bombed it not a little during the occupation, the conquerors, in packing up, are now about to deal the death blow. What are the fish doing, I wonder, near the blockade? Sargo and mullet and gudgeon flitting unsuspectingly around the deadly submarine cables? Despite my mother's urgent pleas not to go out too much on the balcony, every now and then I lean over to see the German in his burnished helmet waiting stiff and still as a statue at the corner. He's the only human being, and his presence enhances the solitude.

Four minutes to twelve: with a joy much mingled with fear I wait, as in a theater box, to see the grand spectacle at the close of the performance. Alien in this city, refugee from the Bulgarian occupation, I don't perhaps feel for her like the natives. . . . Suddenly the roar of a military motorcycle shatters the pregnant silence. The motorcycle, bearing two Gestapo with sten guns bandoleered across their armored breasts, pulls up beside the stiff German guard with engine still running; a few words are exchanged, then it shoots off like a bullet toward the Old Town. Two dry gunshots ring out from above. One of the two riders, we later learn, was killed by our own people, and the Germans, in reprisal, wiped out fifty hostages. "Come inside, come inside," calls my mother from the dining room. But crouching there, I can't get my fill of watching the German standing stiffly below, now looking at his watch, now throwing a glance up and around—only then do I duck lest he spot me—now resuming his statuesque stance. He strikes me as implausible and surrealistic, all ashimmer in the feast of the Sunday sun, a creature from another planet posted there to nourish my avid childhood fantasy.

Three minutes to twelve: all still suspended in a state of trance. Not a breath of air stirs from the direction of the bay, as if the sea by instinct had ceased to breathe. The streets, usually coated by shoppers with a veneer of vitality, are now mute and deserted, as in dreams. Louder and louder I hear my heart pounding. "For the last time, will you come inside?" No, I won't. I want to see, want to relish the Wagnerian finale that will afterward bring the calm of resolution. The instruments will slide into their cases like swords and the musicians plod back to their dreary homes. . . . Then suddenly, in the taut silence, a host of images, like birds flocking to roost in a tree by night, recur within me as if I were seeing these parts for the last time, as if it's not just a question of the harbor being blown sky-high but the whole city and me with it. Now, Saint Theodora's churchyard, where we spent the entire occupation playing tag, help, or tabs. Now, all my friends, except one who set off from Egnatia Street with the convoy of Jews, up on the cart, with the monstrous yellow star on his sleeve, not knowing if he was going on a short trip or a long journey. His name was Ino and he always wore plus fours and a peaked cap, and he had green eyes, almost olive. Now, the passage next to A. Tzerides' drugstore, with the smithereens of someone's brains splattered here and there across the walls like lumps in the whitewash. Now, the towering wall, embroidered with shellshot like a Persian carpet, that brought nightfall earlier to the yard where we played. Now, the balcony from which each afternoon a bloated German, to wake himself from his siesta, would toss a live grenade or two onto the sidewalk below, regardless of who might be passing. Now, Kapani Market, where Moses the greengrocer never had time to yell "onward Rommel" along with the rest. And that corner where the egg vendor's stall stood, the man I used to sell paper bags to, using *Signal* magazine for paper and gluing them with lots of paste to make them weigh more on the scales. It was from this same balcony I watched the night of the great blitz when the Catholic church was gutted and half the city yielded to the flames, the sky stained red between ashen palls of smoke and four nuns scurrying down the street below in the small hours, like gulls who'd lost their nests. Now, the sidewalk where I came across people dying at a time when we'd just arrived as refugees from Kavala, fleshless skeletons, unshaven, with monstrous legs, right beneath the corner patisserie window with its syrup dates and rich marzipans. . . . And all these recollections weigh me down, as if I were too young and too weak to bear them.

Two minutes to twelve on all the city clocks: the German below straightens his helmet. This movement of his reassures me. I turn and look into the dining room; everyone on their feet and nervous, pale as inside the air-raid shelter, the women already blocking their ears. I, too, go in, or, rather, they drag me in. During air-raid alerts we didn't feel the same anxiety. The bombs fell unawares. Whereas now . . . What's keeping them? With the paper union jacks ready to festoon fingers and window ledges still tucked away behind the camouflaged radio, while outside the sun smiles undividedly on the lovely city, I can see no meaning in the words on the plaque opposite, on the Charpanti Clinic, QUIET PLEASE. One of our colodgers has a real stroke of genius and opens the windows at the last minute so they won't shatter under the pressure.

One minute to twelve: unable to stand this nervous expectancy, I select a fat pea from the ones I used to use for paste, and while for a second no one's looking I lean out the window and take aim at the motionless German below. I wait till it drops to see if I've hit him, if he's felt the missile, if he'll raise his sten and start strafing the houses in reprisal—as on the night of the blitz, from the ricochet of a similar bullet, I saw Mr. Moskov drop dead on the terrace beside me—when, just as I'd lost myself, a deep rumble rolled out, as if the sea were groaning from her very bowels, a barbarous moan that in four years found no issue, while something like a tectonic earthquate made the house sway back and forth like a cypress, small objects topple from the shelves and smash, the Papyrus classics—the only ones not burned by the Germans in our whole Kavala household—creak in their bookcase, and the doors unlatch. A second explosion followed, and a third. We found ourselves flung to the floor, clutching each other's hands like "ring around the rosy." Crawling between the wailing women, I arrived outside on the balcony and, cautiously raising my head, saw, over the sea, a monstrous black pall all aflame with burning wood and metal flashing in the sun like lightning at night. I leaned out, and just as in fairy tales the German in his burnished helmet had vanished. I felt my body to see if I really existed, only to discover that for the first time in my life I'd wet myself with fear.

All afternoon the explosions continued. Less powerful, yes, but without respite. They were scuttling their ships, moored along the whole length of the waterfront from the harbor to the White Tower. The emboldened people appeared at windows and on balconies, while we daredevil urchins laid ambush in the shrubbery on Aristotle Square and were grabbing whatever landed nearby. This same square that we'd later come to know as a place of pleasure, where the Scots' pipes played on its open expanse, packed now with open-air movie theaters, this same waterfront promenade and bride bazaar from which the little steamboats set sail for Peraia and Baxé-Tsifliki, for us, for the children of the occupation, was the place where we saw the small hulks scuttled by the departing Germans change shape beneath the shallow waters where they'd sunk. Divers might strip them of all their tackle, the fish might take them for rocks, but no one was going to move them. Much like those bitter experiences that the occupation had instilled in us, that changed in shape and form through the years that followed, yet were always there, as if no one cared or no one could any longer eradicate them.

Salonika: Rising from the Waves

Every prisoner has his own refuge, be it a view from the window or a short stroll around the prison yard and a chat with the others. Constant refuge for me from my cell of an apartment was the Old Town above, with its neighborhoods, its squat houses that still retained some contact with the soil through their courtyards, trees, potted plants on window ledges. Where the cobbled streets twisted and turned unpremeditatedly with their whim, meeting by chance, merging, then parting again to go their separate ways like carefree whistlers fading into the distance. This refuge was always curbed by the Seven Towers ramparts, beyond which I knew there was no more. A gate in the wall, like an archway, unveiled the vista of yet another township that I knew didn't extend far, for yonder began the naked hummocks, foothills of Mount Chortiatis, blazoned by the pylons of the Electricity Board. There I'd always stop, before the gateway, until in the army I befriended a fellow from the settlement beyond the ramparts, on the intersection of Agrapha and Angelos Sikelianos "streets," where the hovels lean against the Venetian wall. He introduced me to "Golgotha," Yandi-Koulé prison, the gypsy women, the refugees, the bouzouki players, the yearning of the outcasts from the stately mausoleums where I lived.

But today, after the cold shower of memory that greeted me in our old apartment building, which I'd gone to visit years later, I'd no intention of going so far up, of seeking my friend from the other world. Besides, I'd neither time enough nor whim. I just wanted to take a short breather in the air of the Old Town, to go at most as far as Cassandra Street. So bidding farewell to the janitor down in the lobby, who couldn't tell me enough how much I'd changed, I set off pensively uphill.

The Arch, Galerius' gateway, was illuminated. Farther on, the new pathway of Our Lady of Dexia had almost been completed, while the adjacent apartment block, which they said would collapse when they were laying the foundations because it violated the sacred soil of Our Lady, now reared its seven-story bulk, blocking the view toward the university campus. I entered Apostle Paul Street with the same bliss with which one slips between one's sheets. Gaining assurance with the Rotunda Minaret I branched left and lost myself in the labyrinth of back streets. But, my God, what was this I beheld?

The struggle was growing fierce, hand to hand. Amid the *rat-tat-tat* of compressors, the clatter of dumpers, the steady roar of generators, the workers were toiling upon heroic constructions that cast bare bones across the sky, ousting the squat houses that with Christian humility were accepting their annihilation. The perpendicular assault of the twin cement manufacturers, Titan and Heracles, few had managed to evade, and these were held captive amid the serried ranks of ferroconcrete perpetually proliferating in antiseismic columns. The streets, in disarray from the massacre of the innocents, had turned topsy-turvy with the onslaught of the beast. Mammoth power shovels, scooping huge bites from the Byzantine soil, were leveling the slight slope that until now availed the amphitheatrical disposition of the "solidary houses." Wherever I turned, down whichever alley I dodged, pursued by the hideous scaffoldings, the nakedness of not one of which had they shame enough to sheet, everywhere dump trucks were unloading munitions for the reinforcement of the fray: stone, bricks, marble, cement, sand, and lime.

Taking as base of operations the district below Egnatia Street, where the general staff of engineers also had their headquarters, the apartment complexes were sweeping up toward the Old Town, which was retreating higher and higher, like shepherds' fires in summer. The combat was uneven. Where art thou, Demetrius, "who laid low Lyaios' arrogance"? I wondered. But the city seemed not to intend to follow the example of her patron. We knew about this invasion of old. But now the scales seemed decisively tilted on the side of Cadmus, sower of dragons' teeth, begetter of armed men to the very heights. And the struggle continued fierce, hand to hand. The houses that had not yet been demolished were nonetheless blacklisted on the general staff plans. Were these perhaps like the marks of the return of Zorro or the swastikas on Jewish doors during the occupation, these signboards hung across the breasts of several surviving Turkish houses: NEW RESIDENTIAL BUILDING TO BE ERECTED. APARTMENTS FOR SALE?

But where the cornerstone, the arched window, the inner court, the sycamore, the potted plants? Where the neighbor, the child, the yoghurt vendor, the girl? I turned and looked up at where they'd installed them; packed in their new closets, they portion out the sun like black bread in the occupation, a child calls another child through a megaphone from the balcony, a housewife hangs out her washing across the space between two blocks, an old lady sits on a narrow verdant veranda where all the potted plants from her yard are gathered together. Seen from below, her balcony, overflowing with foliage, looks like the hanging gardens of a modern-day Babylon.

It's not romanticism or nostalgia for the cobbled streets, for the alleyways, for the hideaways of adolescence in picturesque old neighborhoods, when one knows very well that all the sinks drained into the same gutter, which was the street itself, that damp and fumes from chimney flues that wouldn't draw used to choke the rooms. But the mistake that began before the war with the pseudo-Byzantine, stilted apartment buildings on Aristotle Street, that continued after the war with the blockading of the sea front, and that the same occupation black marketeers are now extending uphill, knowing with the self-assurance of only the powerful how to build, ruthlessly violating a whole tradition without the slightest qualm—for no one can say these ill-constructed apartment buildings are at all more hygienic than the houses they've ousted, since light doesn't reach below the fifth floor; conversely water, not above the first—this mistake is inexcusable. But thus I fear I tread on ground with which I'm not familiar, upon which others still less familiar have already trespassed.

With my heart in my mouth lest they've demolished that, too, I head uphill for the café that was once a midway station on my flight from the new ramparts of apartment blocks which then extended only as far as Egnatia Street. I re-enter Apostle Paul Street and, climbing, reach the intersection with Saint Demetrius. The Turkish Consulate appears, as always, uninhabited, with its permanent sentries, the old plane tree, and two constables. The "Tobacconist—Haberdashery—Stationery," "Hosiery Darned," "Petaloudas Threads," the blue mailbox, "Evga Ices: Cup—Cream—Chocolate —Cone—Cassata—Special," while the corner grocery store is ready for demolition. I turn left on Saint Demetrius, which seems constricted by the bulks of the apartment houses bristling on its banks. The "Forty Churches–Diagonios" bus can hardly squeeze through. Name plates adorn the new buildings: Rika Polkou, Dental Surgeon; P. Kynigopoulos, Obstetric Gynecologist; Coiffure Toula. The Ideal open-air movie theater is showing two pictures, as always at close of season, *Bridge to the Sun* and *Fra Diavolo*. A handwritten signboard on a heap of ruins: "After protracted illness I have reopened my workshop to be of service to my most worthy clientele as formerly."

An Electric-Powered Bakery, a Fina gas station casting its sickly green light across the street, people passing, in high spirits before night, treading the sidewalk chevrons as they stroll along, and here it is at last: in the gloom cast by the neighboring apartment house under construction, the café, L-shaped, calm as the eye of a hurricane.

These are the last of the trees, I reflect as I enter the small courtyard partitioned and protected from the street by an iron railing. As damp descends with nightfall, its scant patrons are sitting inside playing cards and backgammon. I go in and order a coffee. GAMBLING STRICTLY PROHIBITED says a sign on the wall. Beside the mirror hangs the license from the proper authorities. According to this, the café belongs in Category 1, under the name "Skopos"—

nowhere else indicated—and its proprietor is Mr. Zachariades, Vassileos. On the counter, a diminishing line of copper cans, the backgammon sets piled one on top of another like cases in the fish market, a Rectifié calendar on the wall, and, opposite, the photo of the field marshal entering Salonika on horseback. The café is all glass paneling framed in dark wood and is shaped like the knight's move in chess. Delicate yet sturdy, as only the genuine article can be—they say the bomb that exploded in the neighboring Turkish Consulate on September 5, 1955, didn't rattle a single pane —it doesn't at all give you the impression of a shopwindow where you want to stand and gape, nor do you feel like something on display or some novelty when you're inside, which often happens to me in the city's other glazed aquariums.

I go outside and sit in the corner formed by its two wings. Here the chairs are coffee-colored with canework, while inside they're black and all wood. Opposite, the dark skeleton of an apartment house to keep me company, concrete sign of the impending end. CONSTRUCTION WORKS and TITAN CEMENTS. The people off for their evening stroll are merry. Those returning home laden with bags, careworn.

The waiter brings my coffee. When I ask him about the trees, he's somewhat taken aback.

"As for the others, we can't say," he tells me. "That one in the middle's very sensitive. You can't rely on it. Touch it and it breaks. Those three sprout on their own, wild, untended by anyone. They grow unnoticed. All three are somehow akin. Though different in leaf shape . . . In the city there are no decent trees. Cypresses, acacias you find. . . . But these are common throughout the whole Municipality of Salonika. With different colored blossoms, you'll find them everywhere. . . ."

I delve into my pocket to pay for the coffee. He watches me with curiosity, taking note. Now I count the marble-topped tables: there are twenty-two, round and rectangular. The trees: fourteen. The chairs piled up in the corner, I can't count. I recall a waiter, by night, closing time, breaking a marble-topped table as he went to wipe it. "A whole day's wages gone." "What're you going to be when you're older?" "I'm going to Italy to study drama." "And what'll you do with your life?" "A white flag for the cosmic truce." "What's your favorite sport?" "What's sex?" "Cavafy wasn't a homosexual." "Is there any evidence?" "As much as you like." "No, don't go any further. Walls have ears and it's a wicked world." "Right, but I'll see you tomorrow?" "Look what it says there." " 'Demolition Materials on Sale Here.' "

Suddenly I hear a din like a compressor. The marble tops are fused in a blinding white light. A platoon of lancers is charging a green meadow. An automatic arm grabs vertical disks and lays them horizontal. Frenetic music from a ventriloquous pregnant metal belly drowns every other sound. I turn and look around me. Pinball machines, neon lights, billiard tables, jukeboxes—they've all arrived. The boxing on a small-screen TV holds the customers spellbound. I rub my eyes. No, no. I recognize the waiter who spoke to me shortly before about the trees. Now he takes a backgammon set and opens it, very very gently, like a dicotyledonous bloom, in front of two customers. I stand up and bid farewell to the café.

Descending Apostle Paul Street, while the new wave of apartment complexes rears gigantic, I choke with suffocation.

Salonika: Between Two
Film Festivals

Monday

Academician Spyros Melas, president of the jury, declares the festival open and recounts personal recollections of silent cinema conventions. Having disclosed he's just nine months and eighty years old, with the abundant self-confidence granted only the under-twenties and over-eighties, he professes his faith in quality cinema. The speaker had previously announced one by one the celebrities here to attend the festival—actors, directors, members of the jury—and the public, craning and leaning from pit and gallery, applauded as they settled into their boxes.

Tuesday

Afternoons are always less suited to film viewing. I rush out, snatch a quick bite to eat. The weather's improbably fine for melancholic Salonika. Dense throngs of those who've not crammed into the Trade Fair swarm through the jam-packed city streets. When I return, just before ten, crushing hordes of eager fans are waiting to see the actors entering the cinema. But this year the stars are absent. Mr. Spyros Melas, for all his fourscore years, continues to draw the loudest applause.

Wednesday

While we carry on, sweltering under the heat in the Olympian —where the screenings are held—the street urchin sets forth from the slums to hawk lottery tickets in the big city. His coach, a professional hawker, keeps a tender eye on him. This reel of the documentary, hot from the studios, ripples the screen like a breath of

75

fresh air. It steams almost, like bread straight from the oven. The hero is now in the city taking in scenes of the frantic crowds tramping the streets of the mini Koraï Street–Omonia Square arena, the capital's Peloponnesian bazaar. The boy's bizarre turmoil, the huge buildings that surround him, the stab in his eyes from the glare of the cold ferroconcrete, and the headless bodies—seen always from his own small height—fall thick and fast upon him like bursts of machine-gun fire. The tree hung with lottery tickets threads its way through the world rushing by and plucking the leaves of his hopes. Later the cop beats up the young doughnut vendor. The doughnuts roll off the tray onto the sidewalk. No one stops. The child cries. Only the spongeseller, girt with a holster stuffed with white and coffee-colored, large and small porous sponges, "sponges, nice sponges," glides through, as if in a cloud of his own, invlunerable to the shafts of the metropolis. Night falls. The streets gradually empty. Until deserted. The lights at the intersection have gone off, leaving the amber alone flashing doggedly off and on, teasing the drivers' vigilance. It must be past one. In a neighborhood of new apartment buildings stand cases of fruit and vegetables stacked ready for tomorrow's street market, which visits here each Thursday. While one by one the middle-class lights go out, the market watchman in his makeshift shack lights a fire to warm himself as, all alone in the benighted street, he shivers with cold.

Thursday

Torpor has set in to a quite alarming degree. In the evenings, after the screenings, I have an intense desire to open a book, to read some phrase that will set my brain in motion. Apart from the appearance of Academician Ilias Venezis and Mrs. Rika Dialyna, nothing occurs to break the monotony of the boxes.

At a press conference held by the Greek-American film director John Monty the following exchange took place: "What's your film about, Mr. Monty?" "Hands raise—hands raze." "Do go on."

"*Hands* stands outside the conventions of time, place, and country."
"Meaning?" "It's *the* picture of 1970." "More like 1929. Have you
seen *Blood of a Poet*?" "No." "By Cocteau." "Cocteau, I admire,
gentlemen." "And the younger directors, Mr. Monty?" "Fellini and
Antonioni." "But what exactly is the theme of your film?" "It has
many themes. Take your pick." "We found nothing to pick from."
"What? The gigolo! There's one of the picture's themes for you."
"But is that a theme?"

Friday
The Vardar's begun to blow. Now we know we're in Salonika,
which without her local wind is like Athens without her tourists.

Saturday
Cinema, like *Classics Illustrated* and *Photo-Romance* in popular
magazines, may well be an art in decline. According to this theory
the painters come first, then the photographers, next the movie-
makers, and finally the television units. We are therefore still
lagging at the penultimate stage. With the Common Market must
come television to bind us optically with the rest of Europe. For
only beyond the ultimate impasse is there any likelihood of passage.

Sunday
Last day of the Trade Fair and last day of the festival.

Monday
Now the Trade Fair's closed and the crowds have deserted the
streets, Salonika's regaining her real self: her precious melancholy
under uniform clouds over a leaden sea. In the evening at the
ball given at the Officers' Club, Academician Spyros Melas, now
eighty years, nine months, and eight days old, awards diplomas
and medals to prize winners, present and absent. The Italian
orchestra strikes up in a vain bid to thaw the icy atmosphere.
Formal and informal dress intershuffle across the dance floor,

shoulders revealed and concealed, flats and high heels, wing collars and cravats, lights off and lights on, though preferably off, the better not to see the sullen faces.

After midnight in the Doh Ray all-night café sit journalists, actors, directors. The climate here is even heavier, and as bitter as the coffee I'm drinking to clear my head.

100 HOURS IN MAY

(Title of the banned documentary by Demos Theou for which this text was originally intended)

One night in May 1963, in Salonika, a three-wheeled motorcycle, license number 49981, ran over Deputy Gregoris Lambrakis.

The medical examination certified intracranial lesions and contusions of the cerebral stem. Clinically Lambrakis is dead.

The papers speak of assassins. Of the assassins' liaisons. Of perpetrators and instigators. Of national organizations. Some described as "undercover." Text accompanied by pictures. But what are these "undercover" organizations? And who hatched them?

In September 1962, by government mandate, Inspector of the Macedonian Constabulary General Mitsou decorated veterans of the official national resistance for their services to the fatherland. Among them persons condemned in the past as quislings.

Charts bearing skulls. The year 1957 was a landmark for the nationalist organizations. The old, which had lapsed, were augmented by new: National Panhellenic Crusade; National Socialist Thrust; National Socialist Action.

Common characteristic: liaisons with Security.

Common motto: All for the Fatherland.

Sharing these and their views with Occupation Premier Rallis' Corps of the Nationally Minded.

Even children are incorporated. They must be initiated at a tender age. "Children are the prime stuff of the future," said I. Metaxas, likewise premier.

These organizations also comprise militant sections. They wear a uniform with the skull as their badge. Their members are trained to confront the Communist threat. Rather like the Rheims battalions. At the home of one "nationally minded" youth, a whole arsenal was uncovered.

In December 1962, the Undersecretariat for Security styles these organizations "national" and the Minister of Education issues a mandate for a march-past of some of their sections on the eve of March 25.

NMA. Neo-Nazi Movement of Athens. Branch of the Neo-Nazi Movement abroad, as of the Ku Klux Klan.

In 1958, at Katerini, the League of Combatants and Victims of the so-called National Resistance of Northern Greece makes its appearance. In command of the league is National Socialist leader Mr. Xenophon Yosmas, who served as second lieutenant in Hitler's armed forces.

In 1960, Mr. "Von" Yosmas transfers his command to the suburb of Triandria, Salonika.

League headquarters: the Six Little Pigs club. Its ideological organ, the newspaper *Greek Thrust*. Member of its militant section, one Gotzamanis, hauler by trade, driver of three-wheeled motorcycle, license number 49981. Along with his partner and in-law, Mr. E. Emmanuelides, a character with a considerable police record and passenger in the three-wheeler at the time of the accident, he is charged as perpetrator of the crime.

Instigators: Superintendent of the Triandria Security Branch Mr. Kapelonis and National Socialist leader Mr. "Von" Yosmas.

Charged with breach of duty and complicity in premeditated homicide: four more officers of the constabulary headed by General Mitsou.

In 1961, the right-wing ERE wins the elections. Documents come to light: trees and dead men voted.

Leader of the E. K. Center Party Mr. G. Papandreou denounces the government as illegal and declares "unyielding combat."

The government replies with force.

Intermittent clashes with the police. Such is the confusion that police fall afoul of police.

And deputies are manhandled during demonstrations.

Gregoris Lambrakis appears in politics for the first time with the 1961 elections. He emerges as independent deputy aligned with the PAME Democratic Union.

1963. Holy Week. At the atomic base at Aldermaston, England, a peace march with world-wide participation takes place. Lambrakis takes part with the Greek deputation.

On April 22 of the same year the Peace Committee and the Bertrand Russell League plan the Marathon of Peace. The government bans the march. Thousands of people are barricaded at the Ambelokipi end. Lambrakis makes the march alone.

One month later, May 22: The Salonika Committee for Peace and International Détente schedules a meeting in the hall of the Picadilly Club for 7:30 P.M. Speaker: lecturer at the medical school of the University of Athens and deputy Gregoris Lambrakis.

The same morning a member of the committee notifies the public prosecutor that according to explicit information a special detachment has been organized for the assassination of Gregoris Lambrakis.

The proprietor of the Picadilly accedes to pressure and finally refuses to concede the club hall for the meeting.

The committee, after numerous requests and rebuttals, ends up in the Democratic Trade Union Movement hall, corner of Hermes and Venizelou, on the third floor, some hundred yards from the hotel where Lambrakis has just booked in.

Notice of the change is posted outside the Picadilly.

All Wednesday afternoon in Salonika the shops are shut.

The Union Movement hall is situated in the southern sector of the city, in a district of mainly drapery stores. Wednesdays, with the shops shut, this district is deserted.

But not that afternoon. From early on, outside the building and all around, "outraged citizens" arranged in order of police-department precincts, along with plain-clothes policemen, answered the slogans for peace and détente from the loudspeaker installed on the third floor of the building with their own slogans in favor of war.

Gotzamanis' activities that afternoon are unknown to us. All that is known is that he called at the Fifth Precinct Police Station, then at the Picadilly, where he tore down the notice. Afterward he took a stroll along to G. Sotirchopoulos the cabinetmaker's to tell him he wouldn't be by that evening for the furniture removal as previously arranged. "Tonight," he told him, "I'm in the folly of my life. To the point of killing a man."

And he killed Lambrakis.

FESTIVAL 1963

Monday

Heat. The first drop of autumn rain has not yet fallen to kill off summer.

The festival opens in an antifestive mood. Yesterday's warrants for the arrest of the four officers of the constabulary hold the democratic masses in a fever of manifest emotion. The world rejoices to see demonstrated, thanks to the unprejudiced judiciary, that judicial authority functions independently of the other two as the Constitution of the Hellenes provides. The outraged citizens, on the contrary, have fallen silent. On the street, broadsides are distributed demanding the exposure of the guilty higher-ups, and toward evening of Monday two puffed-up special editions of Athens newssheets are in circulation, informing us that the officers have not yet been detained in custody. President of the Trade Fair Mr. Georgiades proclaims the festival open.

Tuesday

Most high, most mighty General Mitsou . . . your struggles were the struggles of our race, struggles for the survival of the Greek Nation. . . . A few lowly wooden stools, a mortgaged house, an only son, he, too, constable and guardian of the Fatherland, and innumerable most lofty and honorary distinctions and decorations conferred upon you by the Fatherland in gratitude, are, together with your prison cell, the sole rewards of Honor, Gallantry, and Devotion to Duty. . . . General Mitsou gave everything. Now he gives even his personal freedom. The body may be fettered, but the soul NEVER.   —Student Nationalists

These broadsides are distributed by car at three in the morning as, exhausted from a cinematically nonexistent day—with just one exception we shall mention later—we head for the Doh Ray for our cups of coffee. The EDA distributed their broadsides by hand, amid the suffocating bustle of the Tsimiskis Street sidewalks and on deserted streets, while the Nationalists used three-wheelers.

Wednesday

The fine weather continues, and consequently the heat in the theater. Programs flutter like fans. People faint unnoticed. The four officers, according to the papers, are now lodged on the topmost floor of General Security, two to a room. In the morning I happen to pass the spot on which Lambrakis was assassinated. The windows of the club where this first martyr of peace spoke are still closed, some boarded up. Spandoni Street is thick with traffic. It's dominated at the far end by a ladies' handbag shop. The spot where Lambrakis fell is still wet—I've noticed it on the other occasions, months ago—as though even the asphalt at that point were shedding a tear, or like the miracle in Bergman's *Virgin Spring*.

Supporters of General Mitsou gather early at the station, setting out from there to demonstrate their faith in the detainee. "Free

Mitsou!" they shout beneath the windows of General Security. The general, having sprinkled them with flowers, orders them with flatfoot gestures to withdraw.

Friday
The "friends of General Mitsou" have returned, tamed to their rustic labors.

Saturday
Parcels are dispatched to General Mitsou from villagers outraged at his internment. Which the general, via the clergy, dispenses to the poor.

Sunday
President of the Jury, Academician Elias Venezis, and President of the International Trade Fair, Mr. G. Georgiades, award trophies and diplomas to the prize winners and all ends well "on this splendid festive occasion."

"Lambrakis Lives"

(Introduction to an unwritten book)

> Mountains quaked, at peace the lion lay,
> The world sighed and blew the clouds away.
> —Phondas Ladis

And thus he appeared unto me in a dream and spake:

"They killed me on the twenty-second of May, 1963. It was too soon for me to die. I was nowise prepared. The accident had to do with this, not with traffic, as they said in the beginning. Descending the staircase to leave the building, I knew something evil awaited me outside. But I did not falter. Even as a boy I was fearless of danger. If I were called upon to die again, I should choose the same way. For they may have killed me in body, but only thus might they not touch the message my body enclosed. 'The seed that falls to earth, yet dieth not, shall rest alone; yet dying, shall bear rich fruit.' This message would not perhaps so swiftly take on flesh, bone, and blood had they not assassinated me.

"But I have not come to talk about that now. Something else I wished to speak of: that last door I passed through, the door of the building that housed our last meeting. Of that last threshold I crossed before passing into the eternity of your heart. Behind, the wide marble stairs were packed with people imploring me not to go out. An old woman's hands grappled at my back, telling me: 'Gregoris, don't go out! They'll eat you, the dogs! They'll smash you! Wait till the cops come first.' It was the same old woman who later at my graveside cried: 'Awake, Gregoris, awake. We await you.' It was an iron door with a grille that revealed the furor raging outside. Heavy door, border of the two worlds: us within, them without. The door was our protection; they'd never dare force it. I knew, as the old woman kept saying, I ought to wait. Yet what

would that signify? With the experience of so many contests in my
life I couldn't remain long in the locker rooms. Outside, the stadium
was bursting with war cries. The fasted lions were hungry. The
praetors' measures were taken. The crowd craved bread and the
dilettantes, spectacle.

"But the door enthralled me. It exerted over me the enchantment
of a prow scudding over the seething, spuming waves. I felt the
same vertigo facing it as I felt gazing at Anaphiotika from the rock
of the Acropolis, proud ship shape, summoning me to the leap of
death.

"I speak of the splendor of this door that was there for me to
pass. Through its grille light filtered as through stained glass in
church, in iridescent tints, tendrils that bind us with the infinite. If
I feared the Roman arena, if I lacked faith, this door would become
a trap door. It would acquire within me metaphysical dimensions.
It would crush me, as cowards are crushed by the suitcase they
carry all their lives, never daring to open it.

"Two or three people hastened to step in front of me, to protect
me. But I thrust them aside, because they marred the glorious
vision of a life entering life through the gate of death. Afterward
it was said my comrades didn't cover me. They even accused fellow
travelers of peace of having proved unworthy of their mission.
Mean conjectures, of meaner stature. For the door bewitched me,
like the Tumulus of Marathon, which alone I descended en-
shrouded in Greece, crucified on the vault of heaven with the
nails of their faithlessness. The door was like the tape at the end
of the race, which I wanted to be first to break with my breast. Now
in the same way I wanted no one to surpass me. I wanted to
open this door—the portals, the portals of wisdom let us enter—
with my own hand.

"I'd exhausted, as you know, all lawful means. I demanded the
representative of law and order over the loudspeaker. No Pilate appeared. I asked them to understand that what I was doing I was
doing consciously and not in ignorance of the legal consequences.
For sacrifice made at random profits no one. They may have killed

me by chance. But I died knowingly and wittingly. I knew as I drew the bolt of the door that I was handing in of my own accord my pass out of life, or what the others call life and which most times is no more than a deep sleep punctuated by the reverberating tones of nightmares. Never was I more alive than I am here, here in your hearts."

Peace Offering
Second Marathon March

An unquiet sun, red, through clouds that yet retain something of the blackness of the Karamanlian night . . .

I've seen many dawns and once wrote hymns in praise of this first kiss of day upon the wakeful brow of heaven. But the like of day dawning over the march, I never chanced to see: cloudlets that soon began to steep themselves in the blood of Lambrakis. The sun came up, and the blood became light.

Concealed amid the leaves of a wild fig tree near the Tumulus, transformed into a tree, I behold this endless unfurling of human faith in a better tomorrow. The faces all seem transfigured with the grave consciousness of their mission. Faces of navigators or crusaders. Faces of first Christians . . .

All regions are present. Vertebrae whose conjunctive links are precisely the gaps that exist between them. Each carries a makeshift banner. Cherubim. Liturgical psalmodies. It's morning and the day before us.

In what way does the peace march differ from an antique or Byzantine religious procession? The saint is with us: Gregoris Lambrakis. Is it not his own miracle that this road which last year he trod alone is this year teeming with thousands upon thousands of feet? In what does it differ from the miracle of Christ, who fed the multitude with five round loaves and two fishes? The icon saints weep tears, they tell us. But then the asphalt on Spandoni Street, where they killed him, weeps constantly. Doubters need only go see: there, at the spot where he fell, the tar weeps. Or our eyes weep, which is the same.

We join the tail of the agelong line—a wellspring, the Tumulus of Marathon, that never ceases gushing limpid water, water of life, into the road, its channel. With us a woman who served ten years as a political prisoner, very wasted, very weak to be hiking so many miles on foot. But I never in my life saw eyes more beautiful than the eyes of this woman, seeing the world on the march and spotting now and then among the anonymous mass fellow prisoners of hers, embracing them at length as they kiss and weep.

A truck overtakes us. It's the Themelio press on wheels. It, too, moves amid the river, urged on by its impetus.

We bypass trees and olive groves and vineyards and fields and the American base, where, white as gulls, its scant Sixth Fleet seamen have gathered to watch, as from a desert island, this endless unfurling of the mute human sea. Familiar and foreign, strangers and friends are the red and white corpuscles in a singing artery suddenly become a vein of the heart. My footfalls recall another march, in New York: in a vast covered space, at Madison Square Garden, some 40,000 people had rallied to demonstrate their faith in nuclear disarmament. On a floodlit platform stood the evening's speakers, officials of the Movement against Nuclear Rearmament, the late Eleanor Roosevelt, Harry Belafonte, other entertainers. When the program was over, this whole encaged throng, with faultless discipline and order, poured into the streets of New York to lodge a petition with the UN. Striding along in line I saw about me skyscrapers towering, gigantic, into the night, heard beneath my feet the rumble and groan of the subway, and told myself that this march was in vain, because Johnny might fear the beast but the beast hasn't the slightest fear of Johnny. The people seemed like ants beneath the sole of an enormous giant who could crush them at will. Around me, within me, everywhere, I sensed fear propelling the feet.

Yet today, in the spare landscape of Attica, where the olive tree accords the measure of the man and its green foliage the color of his hope, this fear is unknown. Here there are no "beasts," and the thirst of men to live like human beings has but one cause: all around, everywhere, the sea and the trees and the sky all speak of peace. This is the best response to the nonsensical bleatings of those who claim such marches have their place only in countries armed with nuclear weapons. On the contrary: such marches have their place in countries still capable of showing other peoples the measure of man, of man not yet annihilated by the machine, nor yet one of its spineless accessories. If the whole world could see via Telstar how the faces harmonize with the landscape, how like are the arms to olive branches, how far the placards from the helicopters ...

But the sun has already hidden behind the sullen clouds of democracy, certainly nothing like the Karamanlian night, though they still do not allow the broadest dawning.

The Houses with the Holes

The houses with the holes are slowly disappearing, he mused as he walked alone along the street, back from his boring job at the office. Those old two-story houses with the faded chocolate color full of the bullet holes of another era. It always bothered him to see them. They always reminded him of sailors' skin tatooed with mermaids. Or of the lame in the street, blind men with an accordion. The sight of them always bothered him because it reminded him of something he wanted always to forget.

He had been a small boy when these houses were riddled with bullets. Small boy in another city in the northern regions of the country. He'd hear the others talking about them. From boyhood he had grown up amid a dialogue that didn't concern him. And he had always wanted to tell them, "Enough. Stop it!" He had always wanted to sing them that inane song he used to hear on the radio, "The world has changed, times have changed. . . ." But they had had their machine guns at the ready and were now no longer riddling these houses, but his own body.

Time passed, and the machine gun of one faction decided to fall silent. Taking timely stock of the change and a leap across the years he found himself with some slight fondness of memory for his dead loved ones, close to the young branches of the burgeoning trees. But then something odd happened: instead of the other machine gun falling silent, too, it resounded more distinctly in the silence, literally howling, night and day. Whenever he turned on the radio, whenever he read the paper, it rattled rhythmically, with the clatter of the sewing-machine needle—rattled, sang, chanted the same bothersome refrain of the Communist peril.

Alone and unprotected he was in this slaughterhouse of a world. He well recalled that slaughterhouse on the seashore, surrounded with pines and fig trees, that was always staining the sea red with the blood of the animals. The others would go fishing on the open sea for gurnard and gudgeon, but he, as he well recalled, had always seen the slaughterhouse, in the setting of the island, as somehow more sinister when devoid of men. At least the men, the slaughterers, and the livestock they were transferring from the pens, had given it a semblance of vitality. But closed up like that, on the point of the squat headland, rectangular, enigmatic, it had literally turned him over. Hence the world had taken on within him that repugnant cast of the closed slaughterhouse by the seaside urinals of the fishing village.

He had quailed, withdrawn within himself, scowled. The machine gun rattled like a cicada in the crucible of summer, clattered like an air hammer when they're digging drains in city streets. Firing the steady volley of a gunned motorcycle racing, hurtling to cannon into and kill on the neutral asphalt a Man who wanted to speak out for mankind.

Then his conscience had rebelled. Within himself he had said the great No. No to his fear, no to his blind faith, no to his parrotings. For his fear had opened the way to the phobia of the others. His blind faith, acquired in the turbid waters of a pseudobourgeois society, had justified the blind failings of the others. His parrotings were proof to the others they were right. His withdrawals from the Moral Savings Bank had drained his credit.

Without delay he had gone and enrolled in the Lambrakis Youth, which was the tree burgeoning on that dead point of the asphalt. A tree that had swiftly spread its branches over sea and mountain, filtered through the irrigation ducts of the plains, wound like ivy around the old plane tree in the village square, ended up embracing a whole generation, his generation; for the blood of the slain martyr had splattered strikers' white shirts, and there he had seen poppies blooming.

Yet there still remained the few odd houses he saw in the streets. Those houses with their scarred faces that hardly helped him forget. And he wanted the blood of his own dead to suckle, not the blood of the others. Despite the flow of blood from generation to generation, like light passing from stratum to stratum, like milk circulating from teat to teat, each newborn babe like himself wants to drink of the blood, of the light, of the milk of his own generation.

Now, one noon like all spring noons, he was walking, heading for home, oddly warped amid the civic concrete and steel. He saw this old khaki house disabled, wounded, dulled like a political prisoner released after twenty years behind bars; and he felt sorry, but at the same time wanted it swiftly replaced by a new house, a house built by young people, with windows open to the hoarfrost of dawn, foundations kneaded with the sweat of the young, squared with the faith of an irrefutable rationale, structured on the new concepts of architecture, of life until then scattered, founded on the inviolable principles of justice on earth, equality on earth, of the earthy tempo of daily bread, a cock having first been sacrificed upon its founda tions to brace it firmly, in accordance with the ancient customs of his ancestors.

A Debate with the Lambrakis Youth

EDUCATION

Now take the young lad who's just left high school with a vague sensation of he knows not what—let's catch him at the moment when with upraised hand he intones the student's oath, at the same time feeling the stubble sprouting with new vigor on his chin, from the very moment when he feels he holds a more responsible position in the world to which university constitutes the anteroom. He's an undergraduate at last, and his sudden unleashing from the tight high-school timetable charges him with that extra feeling of freedom. Yet what happens? Irrespective of what he's reading and his rate of progress, the first thing that strikes him is the bitingly cold climate surrounding him. No one seems to count him as an individual. He's just a number, as in the concentration camps, shuffling from hall to hall, joining the line outside the registrar's, squandering his father's money on his tutor's latest "compilations," reprinted yearly in enriched editions; just a number, clutching an anemic record book incessantly inked in with initials, palpitating outside the viva voce crematoriums as if they were summoning him to present himself each time before the firing squad, struggling through compulsory crammers' courses without which he hasn't a hope in hell of passing; while his professors, those personages he'd beheld at his oath taking enthroned there in their gowns like the Supreme Tribunal of Inquisitors, now, in their everyday clothes, slip further and further away from him as time passes, finally reduced to figments of his imagination. Talking about them with his classmates is like talking about the moon. When d'you think the first cosmonaut will land? What'll it be like? Will there be life or will it be a bleak uninhabitable lump, like metal? This is how the professor comes across through the entire session as he hears him teach ex cathedra, preach ex cathedra, pun ex cathedra, as if the lecture were something to be delivered only ex cathedra. When at last he beholds him face to face in the tutorials, our young student is panic-stricken to find the moon has human features, a scratch on his cheek from his morning shave, eyes, too, that stare at him, expressionless and indifferent, like eyes in the portraits in municipal picture galleries. He notes, with something of a shudder, that they're not interested in his opinion. Coefficients of his failure/success are the street noises outside, the previous quintet to emerge, and his talent as a parrot. So he comes back mostly having photographically memorized the "compilation"— just tell him the page and he'll start quoting the whole passage— while the examination fees pass in toto into the professor's pocket to buy him more and more apartments.

Still sweating from the fever of his degree exams, before he has even had time to air his room grown sour with study, come the implacable tongs of military service to dump him in front of a draft board. "Where logic stops the army starts," rants their drill sergeant. But did the "logic" of his former life come to a halt, or is he now simply passing from one absurdity to another, drawing not a breath in the interval? The awful sense of wasted time begins to rack him. The two years he'll serve form an unbridgeable gulf between what he's been taught and what he'll be called upon to do. They send him to guard the frontier, and he feels that within the territory he's guarding he could be doing things much more useful. Is it not equally absurd that his whole education has been geared toward living in a world at peace, since they never said a word about war, and now all of a sudden everything's turned inside out? No, they tell him. You grew up, you studied, you've come of age, simply so you may one day face the eventuality of war. "You've been on deferment," the regulars tell him, "just like Master War. Sometimes his deferment will be up, and he'll present himself. Otherwise, we're done for. We'll get no promotion and no decoration. We'll stagnate for eternity in the putrid waters of peace." His national service may well run its course without any such occurrence. But the worst of it is they don't hand him, as before, his army discharge, but his marching orders tantamount to a long leave, perhaps the longest he's taken since the day he enlisted. With road, rail, and boat tickets stapled to his orders he has but to await the moment when they call him up again. So he comes to the distressing conclusion that he was born, grew up, sweated through his education, has suffered, and been broken, simply in the end to be allocated these marching orders, sole certainty in an uncertain world, to tie him forever like an umbilical cord to the khaki.

So he arrives on the threshold of real life where he, too, must earn an honest living. Here a fresh hierarchy. A new order of things. The schoolmaster succeeded by the obsessed high-school teacher succeeded by the invisible university professor succeeded by the captain are now superseded by the hard-to-please employer. While he, graduating from pariah pupil to phantom student to anonymous soldier, is now hard up for a job. Qualifications? Twenty-five years' uninterrupted misunderstanding. Age? Prematurely senile. Married? To despair. Special peculiarities? Stigmata. Color of eyes? Tar, almost pitch. "Unfortunately we have no need of you. Your sort are a dime a dozen."

Doors open, doors close. "No vacancies." Day breaks and night falls. "Unfortunately you haven't specialized in anything, apart from bemoaning your fate." Month in, month out. Floors up, floors down. He winds up unable to say what he stands for. Meanwhile, the years are flitting by, and if he hasn't by now fled the country, a certain somebody will crop up, a deputy or someone with pull, to put in a personal call and get him fixed up somewhere. They may even grant him the great favor of a chair in an office, a small office in a big building. His gratitude toward his benefactors knows no bounds. Yet why did they never tell him he'd grow up and study simply to beg one day, the alms of a job? Of so many hands he's passed through why had none the guts to tell him that in the end he wouldn't be needed? Through all adversity, deep down, he still believed he'd be indispensable to others. But these others, rocks for years unbudging from their snug wormridden potholes, show not an ounce of confidence in the young man. Hideously duped, he unconsciously begins serving the grand delusion.

Descendant of an ancient civilization, product of heroes and demigods, grandson of our glorious Byzantium, child of the Greek War of Independence, practically eyewitness of '40, tramping the dust of a country once a cradle of civilization and now teeming with tombstones, he knows only too well he is heir to ancestral death. He arrives all alone at a bitter definition of his homeland that has no room for him: "Greece is the land where all who leave with longing yearn for home, all who arrive with heartache yearn to roam." What put him off at high school is a pervasive atmosphere he now sees well and truly rooted in society. The fault there looms gigantic here. Today becomes a trap door cutting off his air supply. Twice a year everyone pays homage to yesterday. But no one pays homage to the remaining 363 days. Those 363 nails that fasten his coffin more firmly. In a country once a beacon of civilization he feels the loneliness of the lighthousekeeper. And as summer draws on, he feels the legions of tourists marching like ants over his own cadaver.

BEING A WRITER IN GREECE

Writing has always been considered a side line in this country. Mr. So-and-So was a lawyer, doctor, bank clerk, civil servant, and in addition he wrote. Or he had so much money from legacies and property he had no need of a job, and he wrote. We'll ignore the second case, since it's exceptional, and examine the first.

To hold down another job and at the same time write signifies from the outset an attitude of defeatism. You accept a priori the impossibility of living off your writings and resort for your livelihood to some other employment, without, however, renouncing your ambitions. This attitude means that writing becomes a private affair; it loses its organic link with the author.

As a consequence, a man writes to please himself or for his own private relief. Many are the things that smother him in everyday life, so of an evening he steals a few hours from the peace and quiet of the family hearth and writes, allowing, as he believes, his true self to speak. But why is the self that writes by night true, and not the self that lives by day? By what yardstick do we call our rejects true and our life false? Since this man hasn't the courage to contend with the lie of his life, as he admits, he can't write about the sincerity of his feelings. Everyone knows that between what I do and what I'd like to do yawns the abyss. Art is, as it set out to be, still a social function, a public mode of expression, whether or not we've turned it to private use.

So the poet plays the dual-personality game. He metamorphoses into a hedgehog in order to protect a pin point of light. At his office, at his job, no one must know he writes poems. He isolates himself, withdraws into himself. He corresponds with confrères; they exchange books, wind up speaking a language of their own, a language the unversed can nowhere study, because it isn't taught in any of our numerous foreign-language institutes.

In a society still unformulated, like that of Greece, the prose writer finds himself at a disadvantage. For prose—as Lukacs demonstrated in his *Studies in European Realism*—stands in direct dependence on social conditions. Great writers like Dickens, Balzac, Dostoevsky, Proust, Joyce, Faulkner, et alii crop up only in great societies boiling on the brink of great upheaval. In Greece, where society in this sense has never existed and is never likely to, the novel is a form barred from the outset.

Two forms of prose writing alone can bear rich fruit in our present position: the novella, or short story; and the testimony—the eyewitness account, reportage, documentary. Even so, these forms of prose writing, in order to attain some degree of universal stature, must be as far removed as possible from the pernicious heritage of ethnographical accounts. In the world of today the description of any situation—hunger, hardship, taboos, torture—belongs almost exclusively to the cinema. What I think the public now demands of a writer is his speculation on this situation, the essay, disciplined thought, the theoretically equipped insight of the authentic author. The days of the fabulists are over.

If we accept the view that the history of modern Greek literature is the history of the modern Greek language, we have to acknowledge that the majority of, if not all, pre-1930 writers differ from one another not in their ideas or the philosophical schools to which they belong, but in the manner in which each of them uses the language. We younger writers, salved, thanks indeed to them, of the language complex, tend to differ from one another in our ideas and philosophies, as well as our vices.

The writer is himself a helot who may not find solutions or ready answers to all the questions, but who helps clear the fog, helps the reader to an awareness of a situation. He's the cotton gauze with which the doctor cleanses the skin into which he's about to thrust a hypodermic; he's the anesthetic before the operation, the diuretic for kidney-stone sufferers. Such has always been his function in society.

I don't think a writer is duty bound to be committed. It's enough for him to be genuine with and in himself. Committed writers, often without an ounce of talent, will champion some cause in order to find a ready public they could never hope to approach on their own merits. Today, however, inertia on the part of one means action on the part of the other. Your silence is an opportunity for someone else to speak. So that keeping your distance from things is often equivalent to complicity. Not rushing to the aid of someone drowning is tantamount to killing him. Apathy means action on the part of others. Which means many uncommitted writers who uphold their neutrality are at bottom profoundly reactionary.

THE INTELLIGENTSIA

I think the term "intelligentsia" applies to all men of spirit, of *pneuma*, who take a social, ideological, and political stand on the problems of their country and their generation. Their number includes, for example, the political prisoners of every country and every regime. As for that section of the intelligentsia involved in arts and letters, in my opinion fear for our own skins keeps us from getting involved in things that don't directly and personally concern us. Most of us don't concern ourselves with externals until they reach the point, the pain, of direct contact with us. Bad, you'll say. Very bad. But the point is, when the tooth's decayed at the root we can't cure it just by using the right kind of toothpaste.

The intellectuals must align themselves on the side of those who believe in man's future—in other words, join the idealist faction. There are only two factions, one with its own ideals and one that builds its ideals on the denial of those of the first. Now, which faction men of spirit ought to support goes without saying. For the spirit moves, the *pneuma* blows like the wind, presses on, whirls, and aids progress.

In an essay by Panayiotis Moullas, I once read that our word for private citizen, *idiotis,* in Ancient Greek means roughly the same as "idiot" in English and French. For our illustrious ancestors, anyone not engaged in public affairs was an idiot. Now how we've all arrived at being advocates of idiotic justice, that's something else.

Let's imagine a three-story building built like my friend Herakles' brain. On the top floor lives the upper class, on the second the bourgeoisie, on the ground floor the proletariat. I use the public entrance over which a cop and a priest—common denominators in this three-story Ottonian mansion—stand guard. The elevator brings me directly to the third floor. And there what confronts me?

In the first place, I'm a young man thirsty for knowledge, for experience, for life, subconsciously seeking guidance, some orientation. Now let's imagine assembled in this manse representatives of the intelligentsia, the intellectuals of these three classes. We might even imagine my bringing along a manuscript for submission to three such publishing houses. Or even a scenario tucked under my arm to offer to three film companies within these three categories.

Whatsoever the case, whatever the occasion, whoever the caller— if I take myself as an example it's not out of narcissism but, rather, because "I" as a word is shorter and sharper than "he" or "Johnny" or, of course, "Spartacus"—we shall see my observations are valid for all cases.

I make my entrance, then, on the third floor. In the right-hand office, entered by the left-hand door, sits a rather tall gentleman, with long delicate fingers and deep, pained, expressive eyes. He greets me warmly, clasps my hand, compliments me on my new tie, then launches into his grievances about such-and-such a poet or Mr. So-and-So, director. Such decadence in the man, it's oozing down his trouser legs. He works for a rich patron who acknowledges the artist as a kind of opposite—the age-old myth of bohemianism rearing its ugly head in the guise of all the vices. For naturally this man, all sweet talk and gossip, is a pederast. On this kink of his—I call it a kink not because I deem it such, but because he does—he's erected his whole ethos which one might succinctly characterize as a cripple's ethos. The backbone of this ethos? Aphorism: in my weakness lies my strength. Or: in my kink lies the strength of my talent. Crippled by my defect, suffering, I write, I'm a good painter. So talent is drained in notorious hypersensitivity. Vulgar things like ideological struggles, political commitment, a militant standpoint on the exiles, never sully this man's mind. He turns straight to page 2 of the paper, usually the arts page, and expresses supreme contempt for politics. He doesn't serve in the ranks of the church, yet he wallows in metaphysical anguish. Responsibility is a word that springs constantly to his lips, but responsibility as he means it. In the end it comes down to an aging little narcissus who never outgrew his infancy, when his mummy used to singe his backside with a match every time he was naughty.

A few minutes' chatter with this man and I feel stifled. He has a gift for belittling the world, for viewing it through the tight aperture of his kink, whatever that might be. Life is beggared, art transmogrified into a false window—a bricked-in fanlight, the bricks plastered, the plaster limned in superfine sensitivity with the design of the fanlight.

I can't live by such standards. Art, which is supposed to interest me above all else, is not to be manure for my life but dung for my flowers. Of course dung is also manure, but not the only one. I'm weary of the theory that from the dung heap flowers bloom. Flowers bloom everywhere. On barren rocks, in prison crevices. It depends on the flowers. Those in hothouses, sheltered hence rotten, or those blowing wild in the wind and rain?

This type of man claims no interest in politics, so why is he so anti-Communist? Why jump out of his seat at my reply—"*Lambrakis Lives*"—to the classic question, "And what might we be writing just now"? If you were to step straight out of his office into a demonstration you'd be convinced the man doesn't know what he's talking about. That he's living in another world. Where are the despair, the decadence, the degeneration of our times? Here exist men, their eyes ablaze, doing battle, striving for a better tomorrow, like the old man who, when they arrested the whole bunch of us and I asked him what reason he had for demonstrating at his time of life, replied sagely, "Personally, none. I'm thinking of my grandchildren." So this third-floor character is not only extraterrestrial, he's antihumanist to boot.

He's tied to his boss like the crop-tailed dog to his master, who, he says, pays him little, exploits him, squeezes him like a lemon. Yet not a hint of rebellion, of demand for change. On the contrary, he revels in his torments; even these have become consequences of his vices, a *fait accompli* on the part of Helleno-

Christian civilization: from the "Helleno" drawing faith in the exigency of bondage—the aforementioned dung in which alone flowers bloom—and from the "Christian," faith in our sins, in our weaknesses as a bedrock of strength and virtue.

The relationship seems perfectly complemented because that's just what the boss wants. The "artist," the "intellectual," is something "special," something that won't fit into his square gray house, so he keeps him on hand as a confessor—"With your refined sensibilities you'll understand me"—or as a rare bird who drops in of an evening for a little divertissement. The crazier the "artist," the closer he comes to the bourgeois heart, because the more clearly he traces the borderline between them and him.

To the young man who thirsts, who lives through a whole plexus of anxieties, who likes to generalize because it makes him feel he's more into life, this third-floor character is sure to prove quite a comedown.

The windows on the third floor look out on more walls, black, benighted, with smokestacks belching toxic fumes. The sky an endless wall; from it, expunged forever, the watchwords of resistance.

Descending to the second-floor offices, I detect a radical change of atmosphere. This is the progressive intellectuals' floor. No trace of effeminacy in the men, though in the women you may divine hints of a certain masculinity. What strikes you here, in comparison with the top floor, is the earnestness, the good manners, the informed up-to-dateness. You hear phrases that imprint themselves deep in your mind. Art is a thoroughly serious business. Gossip and grievances have no place here. Indeed, these people refer to those upstairs with sarcasm and contempt. All those who enter here, they say, must leave their private grudges on the doorstep, as excess baggage.

People who speak five or six languages, translate, keep up to date, keep you up to date on the latest developments in the Paris School. The world of great writers, great poets, great painters is strictly hierarchized. For the thirsting youth it seems from the outset like the ideal milieu. Despite the feel that this is the second floor, the view is much better than from the third. You can see a bit of sky, a bit of the city, the center, of course. But the windows are shut. Nothing of the hubbub of the street seems to find its way in. At length you discover they're not windows, but superbly executed paintings.

The walls are covered with a world map of the arts. Discuss a book and the other confutes you with an argument to do with painting. Mention a painting and up comes a piece of music to put you in your place. At first you're confused, you don't know what to do or how to account for the vertigo creeping over you. Amid so much culture, so much industry, so much earnestness, so much talent, you feel somehow suspended in midair. All right, you feel like asking, where does all this stem from? Where are its roots? Then you realize it's precisely the roots that are missing, the roots being none other than the people.

Oh yes, the subject raises a storm. The "people" is a concept more abstract than God. So you don't mention them again, but simply ask to stick to books when discussing books and not to confuse the issue with the other arts. Within the vast comparative field in which they move, these people are like children playing on the floor with building blocks, creating improbable combinations of forms and colors, in ignorance of the fact that these blocks were purchased in a market that is subject, like it or not, to the irreducible principle of supply and demand. Whence comes the demand for art to produce the supply? Of course it can't come just from the suppliers. And the consumer, the public? There's the severed root.

They won't preach anti-Communist sermons here. Though they'll tell you they're progressive within limits. What limits? Just one, of course, always. As it's the intelligentsia, freedom of thought and expression. When you tell them that, being free and at liberty in the "free Western world," they can do this or they can do that, they'll come straight back with "we can't, our hands are tied." So where's the freedom? Now they'll tell you they're speaking of relative freedom, while you mean absolute freedom, which exists nowhere. Yes, but within your relative freedom, progressive intellectuals of our putrid world, lies an absolute denial of freedom. While in the absolute denial of freedom of the others, the left, lies relative freedom.

The strangest things happen in this fantastical building in which I've got myself embroiled. I've said nothing yet about the ground floor, where my friend from the other city has his office. The minute you step inside and see him, the face of the world changes abruptly. Though at ground level, through the windows you can see whole villages scourged by disease and lack of the most rudimentary living conditions beyond the pigsty level. You see, as the poet newly born into the world does, dams crumbling from moldering foundations, demonstrations, factory strikes. You can even see the faith of men dying before the firing squad with the cry "For a better Piraeus." You see the figure of Beloyannis with a carnation in his hand. The world is dark, but in the thick darkness lies all the dialectic of the sunrise. You touch points of luminescence which, once welded, would bring "the first sun," as the poet says. Art flees the stifling framework in which the others wish to clamp it, becomes strength, the plow, clothes for the winter, fire to thaw your frozen limbs; art becomes life's resurrection.

While the others are still mourning funerals, here we are just minutes before the rebirth of the world, before its renewed faith in Christ. In this kind of climate you can live. The problem isn't whether to put a period or comma, whether in accordance with Mr. So-and-So's latest work the heretofore generally accepted theory has been refuted. The problem is what do we want to say in this sentence, what does the theory mean? The people milling about outside the house are, in some curious fashion, inside the house. There are no walls of China, no blown-up bridges, no gutted ships. The beaches do not reek of shipwrecks.

At ground level, this floor is in direct contact with the soil. The ferroconcrete roots become boughs from which new shoots burgeon forth. Of course, this is the poorest floor. You can't expect much money. In the fight against capitalism, one must live with and within capitalism. Eliminating exploitation, one must exploit people to exist. But these contradictions are easily bypassed in a broad embrace. The doctor at the battle front can't operate with the facility and means of a private surgery in town. It would be unreasonable to ask it of him. Yet the problem of bread is sometimes so pressing that people who'd like to work on the ground floor work on the second or even the third. Their spirits, their thoughts, remain near to the first. But it can't be helped; the ground floor has, above all, need of hands. Capable hands it lacks, but not all are ready for great sacrifice. Especially not the intellectuals, who are outstanding for love of their own skins.

The second story is the most flexible, and when hard-pressed by the third, ceilings can be seen subsiding and sticking to floors, squeezing it a fraction into the fields of the first. And vice versa, when the wave of outrage wells up from below. This is precisely the floor with no clear contour, hence the most firmly secured. The elasticity of iron is what lends bridges resilience.

Three

Injustice to One . . .

Was the sea ever split into nationalist and nonnationalist? Were clouds ever dossiered? Were certificates of political convictions demanded of trees before they bore fruit? The soul of man is sea, is cloud, is tree. So how can we press it into molds and force it to pronounce, renounce, or denounce? We live in an era of rapidly changing forms and ideas. We cannot allow ourselves to remain forever captives of a slice of the past when the whole of the past is our heritage—our heavy, burdensome, perhaps crushing, yet nonetheless eternal heritage. Instead of seeing it as a totality, we've shamefully isolated it, partitioned it, amputated it from its organic cohesion, the organic cohesion found only in natural silk. After which we cross-examine it, summon it to stand witness before a police tribunal. But the Idea, the heartfelt Conviction, cannot be reduced to a petty offense. Conviction can no more be convicted than it can be unconvinced. Especially today when it's known to one and all that the East-West division is outmoded; who can doubt that it's the same sun that rises in the one and sets in the other? Today we can divide the world only into men of reason and men of passion, into cold brains and throbbing hearts.

For this reason and many more besides, we cannot remain forever behind the times while partaking or wishing to partake of the goods of our civilization. For Greeks in particular there is one danger pure and simple: that we shall lapse into decline without ever having reached our peak. Bound as we are to the chariot of Europe, soon, very soon, our destiny will be one with hers. Europe in the meantime has passed through many stages before arriving at where she is today. We are exactly 100 years behind. Our industry has hardly got off the ground, feudalism hardly been abolished. We have at least two revolutions ahead of us before being born into the rest of Europe's cradle of civilization. Our villages are still ruled by the almighty spirit of Thanos Vlekas, where the peasants, "napes bent 'neath the yoke of bondage," hold their peace. Our cities still bask in the clime that bred Kafka's *Trial*, in which one morning two mysterious policemen arrest Joseph K. in his room without his knowing the grounds or ever finding out, and, despite his innocence, make him bear the burden of guilt for a crime he never committed. Such is the situation. Only in a series of leaps and bounds lies any cure for our ills. Like the leap made in education, like the bounds promised by the present government in the way of lesser changes. Such a leap is essential in the domain of personal convictions. Let the dossiers and certificates of political convictions be abolished to bring an end at last to this rift imposed upon our national life, a rift healed of old in the hearts of men. Radical measures are needed, measures reflecting the spirit of the times, the wind of change. The sands of time flow faster now. And, what is more, each grain of sand counts. Each human being. Injustice to one is injustice to all. Each grain, each human being, is a whole world. "This little world so big."

Political Prisoners

Aegina, 1963. At the end of Aphaea Street, with new homes going up right and left, Aegina Prison, built by Kapodistria's brother as an orphanage with the marble of the adjacent ancient stadium, spreads its stark, slate-gray length, its tiny square barred windows serving only to show that all the rest is wall. At one end stands a police officer with a Mannlicher; at the other, a sentry with a Thompson. In between, beside the iron gate, Prison Security. A couple of plain-clothes men are playing backgammon. As I pass by them I hear the muffled drone of voices from the cells.

Tourists sit outside the island cafés. Mostly Germans, here to view the temple of Aphaea and Saint Nectarios' Monastery and to steal the unguarded icons. All lobster pink and lively, drinking instant coffee, munching macaroons, and relishing the beauty of the island setting.

A mother in black, next to a party of Germans, waits for the ferry. With her sits a child, forlorn.

It's feeding time for the horses, champing their hay from dangling nose bags. With a toss of the head they flick the bag high to get at what their snouts can't reach. It's time for people to drowse contentedly in the languid glow of the setting sun.

Aegina Prison holds 300 of the 1,100 political prisoners still detained in prisons throughout the realm.

The question of political prisoners, recently brought to the fore, has three facets: political, moral, and human. Political because the fact that these men are still being held must serve some political end. Though it's more of a moral than a political issue, implying as it does the problem of choice. Every prisoner's conscience is free to choose one of two paths. Signing the declaration of recantation, he comes out. Refusing to sign, he stays in. Which means that those inside have chosen the latter. Yet no free democratic citizen has the right to deny another his principles, his creed. Much less when the other, for these very principles, is prepared to sacrifice his life. In all fairness we ought to assure everyone of the same creed the same fate. Of all the men who've wound up in jail, why should recantation stand as sole condition of release for some only? This is a partial, the minimum, application of the rules of the game. The correct thing would be all or none. Yet if it's not for their political convictions that these men are still inside, but because they were vicious perpetrators of punishable crimes, then by the same token why is the declaration of recantation not an absolute condition? It's an issue, moral or amoral, not just for those whom, like the first Christians, we make martyrs for not renouncing their faith, but for all of us Romans witnessing the carnage from the tiers. We, too, in our indifference, are responsible for their fate. But despite the moral aspect, the whole issue with all its repercussions on people beyond the prison walls—relatives, friends, families—is first, foremost, and in essence *human*. For while the moral aspect borders on the political, the human element prevails unadulterated in its most tragic form. Is it right, so many years after the civil war, when we're paid visits by Arbouzov and Gagarin, while the Hilton stands watch over us at night, is it logical for veterans of '45 to remain in jail paying the damages for which others were to blame? Neither were we born, nor shall we die molecules of social systems or cogs in political machinery. They baptized us into this world as men with a name, and as such they'll lay us to rest. Just as all executioners are of the same strain, so are all victims, regardless of creed.

Here we are, don't forget, in 1963, in the midst of the springtime deluge of Germans. Most of our factories are German. The Italians are about to install a television network here. Hordes of us have fled to America. And we're just about familiar with the true face of Russia. Can we still be so naïve as to believe, as the idiotic propaganda on the radio would have it, that an unbridgeable gulf exists between the two worlds? Can we go on holding, as hostages of this age-old wrangle, men who forged the national resistance against the invader, a resistance movement revered by every nation but one we ourselves have crushed?

Since visits to the prisoners themselves are not permitted, I went to their homes, to their families for the purposes of this investigation. Spanking new streets led me to slum neighborhoods of the most primordial poverty.

• Saturday afternoon. Sunshine. Nikaia. Two houses, among the seediest in the neighborhood, shacks almost, bear the number I'm looking for. Their one and only shutter closed. Through a narrow yard, under damp washing, a young girl leads me to the mother I seek. A wizened, dried-up old lady in spectacles, her whole body jerking like a half-dead fish. A man stands by to support her, stocky, looking like a blacksmith, although, as he soon tells me, he's out of work. While I'm not paying attention he sends the little girl out for a pack of cigarettes. Shortly after the girl's return I see him open the new pack. He offers me one.

We sit outside amid baskets and tin cans with chickens milling about our feet. The mother, whose son is doing a life sentence, speaks with spasmodic twitches, as if the threads keeping her alive are being severed one by one.

"I'm eighty years old. They've had my boy cooped up nineteen years. They've had him in Aegina two years, and I can't go see him. I'm on my last legs. Think of it, they just grab him and stick him away. I got no home and no job. I'm all alone and miserable, just out of Tzannio Hospital. Three months they had me in plaster. Heart troubles, too. On account of all the worry. What with all I been through. My old ticker can't take it. I see all the children of the world and it breaks my heart. Can't move or go anywhere. Just let 'em bring my boy back to me. That's all I ask. The one who brings him to me, I'll bless him and pray God for his soul. My boy! Just so he can bring me a crust or two for the rest of my days, find me a little room, stick me in a corner. It ain't right they jailed him. It's an injustice. He says so in his letters, 'It's an injustice me being inside.' He fought in the Albanian war. We left here in the occupation. Went to Vertoura village so we could eat. On foot, across mountains and canyons. When he got back they arrested him. Some rat from around here went and said he was with the rebels. . . . We're refugees, son, from Asia Minor. Thirty years ago my husband left me a widow. Turks killed him. Told him he was being taken away to break stones. He never come back. I come here with my daughter and one son. My daughter died in this very room, before the war. Died along with Calliope's girl. That left me just my boy and the government's put him in jail. He fought for his country, son . . . and then . . . aah!"

The man by her side shakes his head with a taciturn, somber, pensive expression. The old lady's eyes are red, but she can weep no more. Her desiccated body's drained of its last drop of water. Her eyes smart, she suffers. She's little more than an overgrown raisin, all wrinkles.

• Tabouria. The house on the main drag. The yard gate padlocked. Shutters closed here, too. A neighbor informs me Mrs. Evanthia has just gone out. Shortly afterward, no knowing how she heard, she suddenly appears, a plump woman, well-built, in her apron. Very agitated. Asks if anything's happened to her child. On learning why I wanted her she sighs with relief. It's not her I want, it's her mother-in-law. Her brother-in-law's the prisoner. Her mother-in-law, an old lady of seventy, was taken into Markomichelakio Hospital two days ago. "One of them two nerves in the throat gave out," she says, "and she's part paralyzed. They got her in 'Nervous Disorders.' "

• Tabouria still. The streets now even narrower, even more bizarre. Either the names have changed or the person I want won't show herself. The man in question's married. The woman tells me there's no one of that name at this address or in the neighborhood. On the way elsewhere through the back streets I chance upon a funeral procession. First come the bearers with the coffin, then the relatives in black; and the farther down the cortege behind the coffin, the straighter the backs. In the rear, the empty hearse.

The woman's not at the other house either. They've just taken her to Tzannio Hospital. Suffers with her legs, her neighbor tells us, drawing aside the door curtain and stepping from her shack. One of her eyes bleary from cataracts. A tin of milk in one hand. She was just feeding the baby, who's bawling and wailing in the darkness of the hovel. "If you want anything particular I'll take a message." When she hears why I've come, her head sags in despondency. "And I thought you was from the Welfare, come to put our names down," she says with chagrin.

• Drapetsona. The street in bad shape but the house large. First large house I've come across. The prisoner's mother up to her elbows in whitewash. She takes off her apron and invites me in. From the window can be seen Piraeus dockyards, the cranes motionless. "Love and Passion" framed on the wall. Tall and lively, fine figure of a woman. She has a Pontus accent, Black Sea area. Her son, too, is doing life.

"I'm driven to the brink of desperation. I chase around everywhere after my boy. Followed him around all the jails. Only Yaros they wouldn't let me go to. I went to Corfu three times. First time I'd just got rid of the Asian flu. Mowed us all down that year. 'Ma,' says my son, 'you got no business being here at all with the flu. If you get sick, there won't be anybody to tend you. . . .' He was a reserve officer in Albania. In the occupation he had a job in fertilizers. One day he says, 'You got to sacrifice me for the country. People can't just shrivel up on their backsides like this with no work.' So he joined up as a leader of the ELAS Liberation Front. He was the one saved the power station and the docks. Cut the cables the Germans laid to blow them up. Then they nabbed him for murder. I ask you, if he'd done it, would he still be alive? Small neighborhood, small world. Everyone knows everyone. How could he have gotten through to the trials, years after? So there I was on my own. No other kids. Makes me

tremble just to say it. . . . Why didn't you let poor Greece go
to hell? Instead you wound up in hell yourself, son, and dragged
me down with you. I was wounded by the German mortars. Had
surgery on my leg. . . . We're refugees from Anatolia. My man
left for America in 1912. Came back to Greece in '31, then left
again. Died in '35, just before I was due to join him. That there's
his funeral. He had money; it was a big affair. . . ."

On the wall facing us a bizarre photograph shows a luxury
casket, all velvet inside like a jewel case. The lid's open and her
husband's laid out in the coffin, two rather squat compatriots
standing over him. In the lower corner of the picture it says,
"Wisconsin, December 1935."

"It was his money built this house. Eighteen years I lived away
from my husband's side. Eighteen years away from my son. Don't
ask me how I lived through the years since my man's money ran
out. Can't read or write, but I have my pride. Eighteen years I
haven't asked anything of anyone. Security police kept taking me
in to ask me what I live on. I work and I live, I told 'em. I go out
cleaning other people's homes. Write that down, my boy. Write it
down, let the truth be known. . . . Better if my son never tangled
with this business. What mother wants to see her son suffer? But
now he's tangled with it, he can't stain his honor. Me, I never
even knew what 'the declaration' meant. Time was when everyone
kept on 'if your son makes the declaration he'll come out.' 'Tell
me, son, what's all this about declaration?' I asked him. 'Ma,' he
says, 'it's the first step toward dishonor. Like you'd be dishonored
yourself when my father left you if you'd taken another man and
got a half-dozen bastards by him. Likewise if I make the declaration.' So I says, 'Son, I won't have no dishonor in my house.' After
that, anyone said anything to me about declarations, I cut him
dead. . . ."

She digs out some snapshots of her son to show me, the most
recent from Saint Paul's Hospital, where he's undergoing treat-
ment. A grown man already, she at his bedside. The warder guarding the bedridden prisoner isn't in the picture.

Some of the commonest complaints suffered by political prisoners: stomach ulcers, duodenal ulcers, hepatitis, tuberculosis, deterioration of eyesight, inflammation of the gall bladder, dysentery, bronchitis, piles, anemia, heart disease, chronic colitis, gravel, quinsy, eczema, psycho-neurosis.

• Nea Ionia. The house consists of one room, with a tiny kitch-enette. Outside on the railings women's underclothes hung up to dry. The absence of the man of the house almost palpable. Inside, an old lady, the mother, and her daughter, a woman of about thirty-five. To begin with, both speak at once, each itching to say her piece. Soon the old lady gives way, allowing her daughter full rein.

"Christos was a mechanic down the Hellenida works. He was no troublemaker. They give us a paper from the works saying he never meddled in strikes or anything like that. But the court paid no attention. When they arrested him, the works paid us his wages for two years. There wasn't any charge against him. The prosecution witnesses, they all told the court, 'Christos, he plays the guitar. . . .' They got 'em all together at the works, time of the uprising, and the ones like Christos who didn't want to fight, they sent 'em to stand guard at the Oulen waterworks. He was with a fellow from the secret police. He and Christos slept in the same bed. Even ate the food I took 'em off the same plate. When they arrested him, the cop came out in the open and says, 'Don't worry, buddy, I'll get you off.' But just my luck, when his case come up and I went to fetch the cop, he was home on two weeks' leave in his village. There was another cop with the same name. 'Ain't him I'm after,' I says. 'I'm after the one who was guardin' the Oulen waterworks.' 'If he's called for the prosecution, okay,' they told me, 'but if he's for the defense, well, he'll be lucky to save his own neck.' The trial was still on when the cop gets back from his village. So he comes down and says, 'You've fixed my wagon, all right. Now I can't defend him.' All the same, he stood up in court and swore Christos arrived at the waterworks four

days after the crimes was committed. So they couldn't make none
of the charges stick. But when the judge asks him if he actually
saw anything during the occupation, Christos says he saw the two
dozen of our boys killed by security cops, in the Kalogreza gully.
That was his big mistake. That's what hit me, sick as I was with
a temperature of a hundred and two and no idea what was going
on. All I remember's the women in black raising hell outside the
courthouse. 'String 'em up! String 'em up! They murdered our
brothers, they murdered our husbands!' In black, and I knew none
of 'em had either brothers or husbands. . . . Then they beat me up,
down by the Megas clock in University Street. Beat me black an'
blue. And me all wrapped up in heavy clothes, middle of June
and sick as a dog. My jacket ends up one side and my handbag
the other. A newsboy come to the rescue. . . . They give us eighteen
years, along with Christos. Every minute he was with us he kept
saying, 'I got sisters. I gotta find 'em husbands.' Since he's been
inside I haven't had a penny for myself. We sent parcels to Yaros,
went runing off to Nauplion to see him, Corinth, Zakynthos with
the earthquakes. Two years now he's been in Aegina. . . ."

"If he come out alive from the earthquake prison," says her
mother, "if he didn't suffer a scratch from the wrath of God,
don't that mean he's innocent? Ah, the Lord forgiveth. Men for-
give not. . . ."

"Three hundred signatures, I collected," the daughter resumes,
"all around Nea Ionia. Landlords, doctors, lawyers, factory bosses,
everyone who knew him. They must have the declaration of recantation as well, they say. . . . After eighteen years, what kind of a
declaration is he going to make now? We told him that right at
the start. Not him . . . We go to Aegina now to see him. They
put him on a diet for his ulcer. They eat a little better on a diet.
We walk through a partition with bars and a double-wire mesh.
When there's a rush there, ain't time to say anything. But why do
they keep him in jail? Why not let him be useful to his country
and his family? It was real crazy before. He had his job, played
his guitar, amateurlike, just starting up—" she takes down an old

photograph from the wall showing a mandolin "presenting arms," in a pose of seated attention before the guitars, Christos in the middle, no more than a young fellow—"and now he's playing guitar behind bars. Teaches the others. The jailer at Hatzekyriakio once said: 'How can a musician be a villain? How can poets and journalists turn to crime?'"

"Wars is all we was born for," says the mother, and tears are brimming in her daughter's eyes. "In Smyrna we suffered even worse. I had four children, all small. One just twelve months old. So I told 'em, 'If you lose us, be sure you keep going where all the others go. Head for the steamboats.' I managed to get 'em here with no father, no nothing. I put 'em in an orphanage for two years. Worked as a cleaning woman, because I didn't have an education. When they was growed up and I was just about ready to say Praise the Lord, my son goes to jail, an' I said Praise the Lord once and for all. . . . This business sows hatred for the government in the hearts of families and friends. Release after release, but the truly innocent stay put. Ringleaders are all out. We all know who they are; cops do, too. If all the criminals are inside, how come all these crimes we read about every day in the papers? The villains are all out, or else the jailbirds grow wings by night and fly out, and fly back in by morning."

The old lady makes ready her charcoal, frankincense, scourers for dishes, candles, all the small wares she hawks around the streets.

"This is what she does," her daughter tells me, "to keep herself occupied, so she won't go off her rocker. . . . My brother, the other one, he's married, settled in Genoa. My husband deserted me, and after all these years I can't even get a divorce. . . . You reckon Christos'll come out soon?"

"If only I knew," I sighed.

What was my crime? On what charge am I indicted? Am I or am I not innocent? When they burned all my corn, when they ravaged my earthly goods, what was my offense? This is the penalty I pay for being weak, alone, obscure, and insignificant. Without favor of the mighty, giftless and guileless, can the voice of innocence gain audience? Hath Justice no eyes? Hath She no ears?

—Pavlos Kalligas, *Thanos Vlekas*

• Perissos. From Nea Ionia to Perissos bus terminal, by the church, thence down Medea Street, alias Lydia Street, where it rises toward the right-angled intersection with Hygiaea Street. In the house, mother, daughter, and daughter's husband. The house mortgaged to the bank, half-built, damp.

The mother, a hefty woman in black with a face like ploughed earth: "He was a cabinetmaker, a good guy, all for justice. His father and uncles were killed in Smyrna. Since '22 they been killing us. Ain't they had enough? Now they're putting us in jail. Who's gonna pay us back our menfolk? Their heads chucked down the mountainside for the dogs to lick. The big shots, the high-ups, they done it all. . . . My son trudged all way back from Albania on foot. I didn't know nothing then about getting papers to make him head of the household. We tossed his army gear up in the loft, then he went to work. All through the occupation he went around in an overcoat from '40. Came down to his knees. We lived in the slaughterhouses. They lied at his trial, said he was a killer, said he disarmed the cops. I caught hold of one of 'em and I says, 'Do you know for a fact my son did all those things?' 'They brung me here,' this fellow says. They pay the piper, they call the tune. What about the other wrongdoers? Did any of them get put away? He's in Aegina now. We're gonna see him Tuesday. They got him in a cell by himself because he snores. Something wrong with his nose. Ten operations he's had, and the doctor at Corfu wrote out an order for plastic surgery. But it's being held up at the ministry. They took him to Kallithea, to the mental hospital, because he suffers with his nerves. Doctor said he's gotta go once a month for therapy. But he's no sailor, he can't. . . . He built those shelves there when he was fourteen. Has a knack. He wasn't a man to go around killing folk. It was justice, I tell you, equality he wanted.

. . . I got cataracts from crying. Can't see. Got asthma and arthritis and all. Write down my ailments as well. They know about
them at the ministry, too, but what do they care!"

She fetches some photographs. On his army record card it says:
Education Grade: Junior 2nd. Height: 5'8½". Conscription Classifi-
cation: 1937. Religion: Orthodox. Profession: Joiner.

"So long, and may you bring us luck! May you bring him back
to us," she says, showing us to the door.

Nearly all said the food was middling, but Thanos was of the few who
testified to the truth regarding its recent deterioration. This incensed the
recorder against him and he counseled the examining magistrate to
teach Thanos a lesson in Spartan living and black broth, prolonging
his stay in prison to eternity. . . . Interred in prison or, in other words,
consigned to oblivion.   —*Thanos Vlekas*

• Nea Liossia. Once more, names of renown to designate streets
of the most abject squalor. Priam, Troy, Odysseus, Iliad. I want the
street of the cyclops Polyphemus. Nightfall.

The house is high-ceilinged like a thatched cottage, but icy.
Father, eighty years of age, is bedridden with paralysis down one
side. He can barely move his left leg under the bedclothes. Mother,
in her seventies, wearing spectacles on a face all eaten up, sits beside him. A visitor, on seeing me, gets up and leaves. Also present,
the daughter and her husband, from Mytilene.

The mother: "We've been here in Nea Liossia thirty years. Came
here for a step up in life, from Panakto, near Thebes, end of the
earth. Summertime, not a drop of water. Six villages, and only one
priest. There was fireworks in the occupation with the Germans.
Twenty of our people killed, but not a single German set foot in
the village. Anybody tried it, he'd had it. Two hundred or so. One
got away wounded, got back to tell the tale, so they come down
like a ton of bricks. Burned all six villages to the ground. . . ."

"How many years since you've seen your son, Grandpa?" I ask
the old man.

"Who knows?"

"We saw him two years ago," says the son-in-law. "I took my wife to Itzedin in Crete. That's where they have him now. Sure, he's done the grand tour of all the prisons."

"How was he?"

"When a man's done eighteen years, how d'you expect him to be? A well-built fella, but rotting away inside. He's sick three or four times over. What help can I be to him now? I'm working in the building trade. Who's to come first when it comes to the wages? My own family? The old folks? Or him? The old man gets 780 drachs Social Security pension."

The prisoner has a bullet wound in the arm from the Albanian war. At Tepelini he held the Bren gun to cover the retreat, with two other men, who were killed.

"His left hand's no good to him," says the old lady. "Can't even tie his shoelaces. He wasn't one of them who joined the organization just to rob folks an' eat well. He was an idealist. When they told him to sign the recantation he said, 'I'm not guilty. I haven't killed anyone. Let them who judged me recant.' Twice he was tried. First time they had him up for murder. Everyone around here knew who the culprit was—Nea Liossia was split right down the middle at the time. He was the council chairman's godson. Second time they charged him with criminal acts in general, on no specific evidence."

The son-in-law: "Nowadays, you see, going to court's a different thing altogether. Nowadays you get witnesses and lawyers. In them days you couldn't stand witness for the defense. Nobody could. And Greece'll never be short of chiselers. Build your house here and the next minute someones comes along and chisels you out of it. Not in them days . . ."

His wife, to me: "You think they'll let 'em out in the end? There's two or three other prisoners from the village."

The son-in-law: "A lot of governments have come and gone, and nothing's happened. Tell me, is it gonna happen now? When it comes to that, every door you knock on at the ministries, it's slammed in your face."

On the table a piece of prison handwork. Extract from the prisoner's letter: "During the Easter holidays a pal of mine will be coming to bring you two crabs, the one with the green cloth for Dimitrakis' godmother, the one with the red for Maria's. You must go along with the kids when they take them so they won't get broken. Will the two godmothers please accept the humble handwork that we fashion here?" Over these words the red pencil of the prison censor.

"But it was the old couple in Nea Liossia who really shook me," writes the friend who went with me. "Heads bowed beneath the burden of an unbearable fate, as I said only yesterday. Then the serflike feeling. There were moments when I thought the old boy was about to whisper in hushed tones: 'It's the will of our Little Father the Czar.' Then something else: at one point you asked the old boy, 'How many years has he done, Grandpa?' He raised his head, gave you a vague look. 'Well, son, it must be fifteen, sixteen, seventeen years. . . .' His voice drawled long and slow, his head dropped like a bird swallowing water. My God, such tragic contempt for the arithmetical properties of time. Its duration devoid of substance, decayed, dramatic, pitiful . . ."

"When you, the masters, will it, all is possible. We prostrate ourselves before you. . . . You shall have our benediction down the ages, to the last generation, as long as Thebans live. . . ."

"Benedictions need censers," replied the chief notable, "and the censer incense. Without incense no saint is venerated."

"That we understand, Excellency! But thou knowest our poverty, how near we are to breaking! . . ."

And bitter tears coursed from their eyes.   *—Thanos Vlekas*

• Peristeri. Like a drop of ink on blotting paper Peristeri sprawls diffuse and chaotic. The street I want isn't known. "Don't know it—I'd send you around the houses." "I'm a stranger here myself." Grocery stores, kiosks, gas stations, passers-by, wherever I ask all shake their heads. At last a kid gives the first clue as to the right direction. . . . And a drunk on the corner pin-points the area to search: the Armenian quarter.

"Despo!" yells her neighbor. "You're wanted!"

A pallid woman, wrapped in a bathrobe, appears. "Come in," she says. She's exceptionally delicate, with noble features. But ghostly pale. She fastens the lower buttons of her parti-colored bathrobe, which only accentuates her pallor. She perches with no real weight on the edge of the divan. On the table a deck of cards which my friend shuffles with embarrassment. As she tells us later, she, too, is from Asia Minor, from Smyrna, actually. She arrived here after the disaster, at the age of two. She never knew her father.

It's a basement room, with another room above, where they sleep. She lives here with one of her sons—the other's married— who was a three-month-old baby when her husband was imprisoned. Now he's eighteen, as many years as her husband's been inside. He's due back shortly, any minute, in fact. The house is a grayish wooden two-story shanty similar to all the others in the neighborhood.

"I've got cancer. So I tire easy. Today I went to do some washing and . . . I just lay down. You see. Two dozen radium treatments I've had. I'm all open here"—she touches her stomach—"my stomach's an open sore. The doctors told me there's nothing they can do. So all I can do is wait."

Outside, on a level with the window, the chickens are driving us mad with their cackling.

"I had a little girl, too. Lost her when she was eleven. Burned to death at the gas stove. On Saint George's Day, ten o'clock in the morning. I was out at work, house cleaning. That was only two months after I got out of prison. I had to live. . . . Yes, I did five years, '47 to '52. They accused me of being oral liaison and condemned me because I wouldn't denounce my husband. A twelve-year sentence, but I got off with five when a retrial was ordered. I was in Averoff, and the Italian School at Patras. . . ."

Soon the son arrives. A fine young fellow, modest and unassuming, shirt sleeves rolled up. After graduating from junior school and the Diesel Technical College, he now works on building sites as an elevator technician, earning thirty drachmas a day. He pays frequent visits to Aegina to see his father. "The visits are a farce," he says. "Standing room only. They'll do anything to bug you. You can scarcely make out the faces through the mesh. And you have to shout when they bring out more than a few. The guards watch you like hawks."

"What do you talk about with your father?"

"Oh, the usual things, you know. The same whenever I go. Advice, family matters . . ."

"What kind of advice?"

"Look after my mother, don't stay out late, don't keep bad company. . . . Last year they let him out for a couple of minutes, and we hugged each other for the first time. That was all."

"If they paid him his wages for all the days he's worked in the prisons," says his mother, "he'd be out by now. But they won't, just to torment them all the more. He only got his pay for the days he worked at Yaros. They gave him twenty years. With the days he's worked, he's made it up to twenty-five. He should've been out long since."

"What d'you mean by his wages?" I ask her.

"When a prison wall needs mending," she replies, "a window or the warden's door, a prisoner's entitled to the work. Then that day's work is counted as a day and a half or two days of his sentence. A lot do it to get out sooner. But all the prisons he's been in it's not been counted."

Silence again. Difficult. A motorcycle draws to a halt outside the window. The engine cuts out in a clattering volley of backfire that drowns the cackling of the hens. The woman, sallow, feeble, buttons and unbuttons her bathrobe with embarrassment. My friend stacks the cards. And the son sets the seal on the conversation. "Nothing else." Yet his voice hides the germs of a different verdict.

"Yet again I cannot comprehend. You have, I hear, a Ministry of Justice. What, then, is its function?"

"Indeed 'tis hard for a foreigner to fathom the ways of the Greeks. Bavarians made our laws, and we abide by them since it is our wont. . . ."   —*Thanos Vlekas*

• Aigaleo. Everywhere signboards advertising EASY PAYMENTS. Children playing with sticks and stones. In the middle of the street, a yellow kite caught up in the branches.

Where asphalt trails off into the dirt of Queen Frederika Street, I spot the number I'm looking for. I enter to find myself in a communal courtyard with the well in the middle, as in the movie *Return of the Germans*. A woman sits by her door knitting. She tells me the old lady I want was admitted to Laïko General Hospital some three weeks ago.

I walk back down the same street I'd walked down a few days previously on the way to a house where I'd found nobody in. But it's now clear that the earlier visit has created a by no means favorable stir. The tidings have been borne amiss to the prisoner's family by the neighbors. They said the father was to be released. Two men, they said, had brought word of it. The daughter, not three months old when her father was imprisoned, delicate, frail, with weak nerves, took sick with joy and trepidation. I find her in bed. When she learns the reason for my visit, an enormous weight is lifted from her shoulders. So many days had passed with no further news, she was almost out of her mind with anxiety. Nonetheless, a deep-rooted suspicion that I'm an augur of doom rather than bliss puts her on her guard against me.

Also present in the narrow room with sloping ceiling, which is all the house consists of, is her mother, here from their village for the same reason. Her head swathed in a white kerchief. Her hands rough, callused like a laborer's. The girl's brother is out at work. He'll be back at two.

"She got terribly scared," her mother scolds us.

"It's not really my fault there was a misunderstanding," I respond. "The girl got hold of the wrong end of the stick."

"What's done's done," she retorts. "Well then, what can we do for you?"

I feel incapable of surmounting the barrier of accumulated terror. Terror has a stronger grip in the villages than in the cities. In the villages the past is harder to forget, and changes, too, come harder; grudges between families, bound up as they are with inequalities of ownership, defy resolution. . . .

"Just talk to me, talk. . . ."

"Talk about what?" asks the peasant woman, withdrawing farther and farther behind her kerchief. "What do we know? Three brothers of mine were killed. One on the front. Nazi collaborators killed the next. Third died in the war. . . ."

"Which war?"

"How should I know? The war Uncle Takis was with him in."

"Asia Minor, she means," says her daughter.

"How am I supposed to remember?" her mother goes on. "They brought reports he was dead. Put the fear of God in us. They beat the life outa me. My heart'll bear witness. . . ."

"When did you first see your father?" I ask the girl.

"When I was ten."

"She was too shy to look at him," her mother chimes in. "Hid behind her brother."

"And another time, when I was thirteen, and they brought him to Hippocrates Hospital for an operation. He kissed me then for the first time, and I truly felt I had a father."

"When did you leave the village?"

"Six, seven years back. I came to Athens to learn dressmaking from my uncle. They still hate us in the village. Animals . . ."

"Considering everything, we've done all right," says her mother. "I can take it easy now. They don't get at me no more. . . ."

"What was your husband's job?"

"Barber. Did the same job in jail. Gave it up now, can't see. Us neither, when we visit him . . ."

"What do we ask that's so unreasonable they keep hounding us?

Food in every belly and our father out, that's all we want," says the girl.

"Know no hunger, know no pain," says her mother.

The keen suspicion that I might be secret police clouds the brother's face the minute he crosses the threshold. A lad who's suffered much in his childhood. They dragged him off to the beach for execution, made him talk about what he believed in, caught him and nearly drowned him in the village well one morning when he was fetching Red Cross milk. All this we learn before his arrival, from his sister.

"Seems you know more about me than I do myself," he says.

Though his suspicion cuts me to the quick, I keep cool. After all, he's not entirely unjustified.

"Best consign the whole business to oblivion," he resumes, "else conscience rebels. Let's stick to the present—prison makes wrecks of 'em all. Can you call a sixty-one-year-old man who can't see a subversive element? You being, so you say, a journalist—we don't even know that for sure—we have only one thing to say: we want our father back. Let him spend his last years with us so he can die in peace in the arms of his family."

"I raised these kids," says their mother, "digging spuds in the fields. . . ." The sister's a dressmaker. The brother works as a clerk. He's a church chorister on Sundays. Goes to the Parnassus Club lectures rather than the movies, and whenever possible reads, reads a lot. His eyes have that unearthly glow of the holy. When I press him to speak frankly, he confesses.

"Sad to say, I've assumed a role not at all to my taste. I'm head of the family with responsibilities I'd rather not have. But what's to be done? Personally, if it weren't for my mother and sister, I'd choose to live quite differently. . . ."

We leave. The detached house next door is a home for retarded children. An imbecile sitting in his chair shakes his head when I say hello and mumbles, "It's gonna rain." "That's all he ever says," the neighbors tell me.

Who is to blame? Hephaistidis, who had faith in the innocence of the good farmer? Or those who lavish amnesties and pardons upon hardened brigands and gallows birds, exerting all the severity of the law against those who by the sweat of their brow earn their daily bread? This state of affairs should seem in no way singular, since the innocent serve as the scapegoat of society in order to hide the shame of the villains' impunity.   —*Thanos Vlekas*

• Pangrati. The only woman who wouldn't see us. Very old, over eighty. The grocer discouraged us from just turning up on her doorstep. He sent his boy along first to sound her out. While we were waiting he had this to say:

"Poor old lady Chryssa, she's nothing but a bag of bones. She hasn't touched olive oil for God knows how many years now. She just eats fruit and boiled beans. Up till last year a few olives, too. This year she won't even eat olives. Any minute she's likely to collapse in the street. Lives like a hermit. I keep telling her to go to the doctor. There's only one doctor for her." And he points skyward. "She believes if her son's survived this long it's because she's a servant of the Lord. Never misses a single service, vigils, evensong, Sundays. Every saint's day of every church, off she trots with her offering. Buys oil enough for a whole family to live on, just for the lamps. 'What's wrong with cheap oil?' I say to her. 'That's just where we need the very best,' she says.

"She's from Andros. Her husband's folks are all in shipping. He was a wireless operator. She belongs to a church and religious society, all housewives and old ladies. Zolotas, him in the bank, his mother's the leading light. There's another woman, well known, Maritsa, from Kaisariani. She goes, and she's the archbishop's favorite because he's from them parts. Old lady Chryssa keeps well away from them protests organized by other mothers of political prisoners. She thinks she'll win her son's release with the aid of God alone. I don't know how saints get proclaimed saints, but they ought to proclaim her one."

The youngster returns with the news that she's not in. Then he says she's in but refuses to see us. She's not, she says, going to be the laughingstock of the newspapers again, like Glezos made her. "She shuns publicity," the genial grocer tells us. "But come back another time. You might find her in the right mood. . . ."

The prison bore the closest possible resemblance to icebound Tartarus. The area below ground level between the two thickest walls of Chalkis Fortress had been excavated by the medieval masons and roofed over with quantities of earth, probably for storage purposes. . . . Into this Erebus were cast tried and untried, together and without distinction. . . .

—*Thanos Vlekas*

• Piraeus. I found the mother in her son-in-law's tailor shop, Saturday afternoon and work at full-pitch. Pants and jackets to be delivered by evening. Sunday tomorrow. So many weddings . . . A thread dangling forgotten from his lips, the tailor kept the heavy iron constantly moving, offering us coffee and cigarettes without pause. Behind the partition his wife, in the pants department with two girl assistants, keeps a sharp ear on the conversation.

The mother begs our pardon for being unable to receive me in her other daughter's home, where I first called on her. "Her husband's righter than right," she quips, stressing the comparative. "We never knew before. After the wedding it all came out. . . ."

"Now show some respect for the dead . . ." says the tailor, leaving the sentence meaningfully unfinished.

The mother, over seventy, is a warmhearted dumpling of a woman from Kalamata. First of all she shows us the sole surviving photograph, blown up, of the hanging of her other son and son-in-law by the Germans in the Tripolis square. The crowd cowers terror-stricken in the background. The two corpses, hung a foot off the ground from the same post, look intact, jackets on, their napes raised slightly from behind. Six more were hanged that day, but the organization got no more pictures because meantime the Germans caught on and routed them out. She was there herself at the scene of the crime. She'd fainted.

"When my boy Nikos, who's in jail now, worked for the re-sistance," the long-suffering mother relates, "the Germans, with all the arrests they were making at the time, went into the café in Kalamata and arrested my son and son-in-law, the ones they hanged. They took them to the camp in Tripolis. December fourteenth, 1943, they nabbed 'em. January fifteenth, 1944, they executed them in reprisal for the murder of a German officer. When I went to see him in Tripolis on the eve, they wouldn't even let him out as far as the wire. A camp committee came out and said no more visits. But I found a boy I knew and he let him come to the wire. 'Mother,' he says, 'tell yourself you had no son. What do you prefer? An honorable life or a death disgraced?'" In her turmoil the poor old lady got it back to front. "He'd be released if he turned collaborator and went around the villages in a truck denouncing Greeks. Volunteers of that kind Peloponnesus is crawling with! 'An honorable death, that's what I'd choose,' I told him. 'Then good-by, Mother. For keeps. Tomorrow we'll be taking a stroll. . . .' Next day they told them they were taking them on a work detail. You saw them in the photo, hands and feet bound, a foot off the ground. My husband passed away twenty-four hours later, of a stroke. And where there'd been four men sitting at my table, I found myself a widow sitting there with five daugh-ters. . . . I cried my heart out. My granddaughter used to say, 'Don't cry, Granny, you'll make me cry, too.' That little tot was balm to my heart. We were poor, but we made the best of it. We had our own home once. The Germans burned us out. . . ."

"And the other boy?" I ask her. "Er . . . Nikos."

"He escaped execution, see, but he won't escape jail. . . . All our troubles started with the English. With the Italian and German air raids, we fled, the whole family, and took cover in the caves around Kalamata. Nikos was sixteen years old then. He says to me, 'Ma, I'm going down to Kalamata to see what's doing. It's a bit too quiet. . . .' That was the time the English were on the run from Athens and camping in our gardens. He came across a couple of Englishmen, who told him, 'We need clothes like yours.' He put them upstairs in our loft, and then, during the night, brought them to the caves, where we took good care of them for a month. And for one month more, with the fear of God in our hearts, at home. Then our godmother—she was an interpreter for the Italians when they occupied the city—came and said the neighborhood was buzzing with rumors we were harboring Englishmen at home, and to be careful. The Englishmen got off in a submarine, but before leaving they wrote down their names and addresses in England on a piece of paper so we could exchange letters when the storm was all over. My son put that scrap of paper in his jacket and later hung it on the wall. When they raided us they found it. My Nikos was a blacksmith. He was working at the time with the Italians, fortifying the harbor. They chased off after him and he fled with his sister to a village in Tifaris. From there he joined the resistance, Elias Karamouzes' brigade. With the liberation he came down with them and surrendered his arms. But the security death squads went after him. He took off again and came to our uncle's, here in Piraeus. Uncle was working for the Port of Piraeus Authority. Three years Nikos worked there. He was forever being picked up on fake charges of stealing groceries or dressing as a woman and handing out leaflets, but he always got off. Then in '47 they arrested him here in Kokkinia. They sent him to Tripolis, then to Yaros till the trial, when they charged him as accessory to the murder of Zervopoulos, the new chief constable just arrived in Kalamata. There was a fight lasted two and a half hours—a battle, sure enough—but Nikos wasn't there. He was here, in Piraeus. In hiding. And a lot more besides. False accusations, I can hardly remember them now. . . ."

"Me," says the tailor, working away at the heavy iron, "I'm from Crete. Only been part of the family since '56. But I work almost exclusively with Peloponnesians, and I know what sorta people they are. I have only two or three Cretan customers. It's my considered opinion, without bias one way or the other, that the boy's a victim of false accusation. Everyone who knew him tells me what a great guy he was. In those days the people were divided, and in Kalamata, they say, things were even worse. One bunch went right along with the Germans—they weren't short of a bite to eat and a drink or two—while the other bunch took to the mountains to fight the invader. And spies everywhere. One step to the left and you'd had it. But to judge by results, beggars stayed beggars with mouths full of cobwebs from starvation, while my wife's family, uprooted and all, pulled themselves up by the bootstraps. The two sisters bought a plot of land, built the house, and now they're living. . . ."

"Night and day I toiled at the loom," says the mother, "to earn our bread. Not a wink of sleep until I had forty drachmas. And my daughters, they worked very hard. Now it's too much for me. I move around from one daughter to the other. Four, I have. My son-in-law here keeps telling me, 'One of these days you'll take a fall in the street an' it'll be all over the papers.' Because when I'm out walking my mind wanders, like; I'm off to one place and end up in another, then I wake up fifteen minutes later and think to myself where it was I had to go. . . ."

"What we want is a retrial," says the daughter from behind the partition. "That's all. With a retrial he'd get off. The widow and son-in-law of Zervopoulos himself told us they'd come running to swear our Nikos wasn't in that fight. . . ."

"Ah," sighs the old lady, "my trials have been heavy and my tribulations great."

Meanwhile, the shop's jammed with customers come for their various garments. Time to go. "Greetings to Mitsos Psathas," says the tailor with the thread between his lips. "We never miss a syllable of his. . . ."

Many of those formerly prosecuted, in accord with this train of thought, in line with this political end, or, in plain language, loyal to the same system, were granted amnesty, favors, and high office. Among them Tassos, who was not only pardoned, but in addition promoted to the rank of lieutenant. . . . While poor Thanos, stripped of all he

possessed, had no chance even to defend himself. . . . The contrasting
fates of the two brothers seemed unaccountable. . . .

—*Thanos Vlekas*

• Piraeus. The prisoner's wife in bed with a slipped disc. Four
months now. A refined face, delicate, with olive-green eyes. Her
blood's been boiling all morning after Minister Averoff's announcement that our prisons hold no more political prisoners, only
criminals convicted under the penal code. I seem to have arrived
right on time for her to pour her heart out and to cheer her up
a little.

It's a prewar house, big rooms, high ceilings. Shyly at first, two
other women, a young lad, and a toddler congregate at her door.
Then they come in and sit down, and together we make up a
family. They, too, I learn, are victims of the resistance.

"Did you hear what Mr. Averoff said about no more political
prisoners?" says the invalid. "What's my husband, then? They
picked him up in Mytilene in 1950, along with sixteen others at a
meeting. He spent twelve days in the police station. 'Sign,' the
chief kept saying, 'and you're free.' 'Why should I sign?' They
locked him up. At the trial, sixteen of them were released because
they signed. My husband got twenty years for being a dangerous
Communist idealist. He left me a baby, five months old."

Her son, a sturdy lad of thirteen, leans back against the open
door with an odd gaze in his big dreamy eyes. Like his mother,
he has very aristocratic features. He could be the scion of an ancient
patrician family.

"My husband was a stranger in Mytilene. We speak with an
accent of our own over there, so he didn't understand too well what
was being said. So, you see, they picked him up as a stranger, a
suspicious character. Nobody knew him. We were married here
in '47. He was a cobbler by trade. My father died in '50, in Mytilene.
My brother was doing his national service, so we went there to
keep my father's café from closing down. One day he tells me
he's made friends with a couple of boys from security. He was

happy; I was happy. We didn't have any cause for concern. But there was cause enough for them to keep an eye on him. Not a month passed and he was arrested. Two cops stood up for the prosecution and said he had no business being in Mytilene, he was sent by the commies. It was all my fault! If I hadn't dragged him off to Mytilene, we'd be sitting pretty now. From then on, I've been going steadily downhill. I was a laundress in other people's homes until I got this spinal arthritis and a slipped disc. Now it's just my son works, in the machine shop. They were giving him sixty drachs a day. Now he brings home seventy. . . ."

The other women beg her not to get excited, to keep her voice down. The invalid struggles desperately to raise herself from the pillow but keeps sinking back.

"This poor boy only came to know his father three years ago. They were transferring him from Alikarnassos to Amphissa Prison. He sent us a wire. Friday evening: 'Am at Athens Transit Camp.' He'd be there just a day. Saturday morning we started off. The guard wouldn't let us in. I told him I hadn't seen my husband in ten years and my son was going to meet his father for the first time. No dice. So I went straight to the warden and begged him to let us see him. He gave permission. I had to see about a parcel. My boy went in on his own. He looked hard but he couldn't make out which was his father. His father spotted him but didn't know if it was his son or some other prisoner's boy. So he got a pal to call out his name. My son glanced up and he ran over and threw his arms around him. When I arrived, I stood back and watched them gazing at each other. 'Let me do the honors,' says I. 'They're done already,' says my husband. After that he wrote me from prison, 'I'm overjoyed to have met such a serious lad.' After all this time we've got into the habit of discussing things cold-bloodedly. Like a bit of gossip about other people."

She pauses. Takes a deep breath. I light a cigarette. No, the smoke doesn't bother her. The older woman smothers a sigh.

"I always wanted a girl," the invalid resumes. "So when the boy was small, I let his hair grow in long blond curls. How I loved

them! I'd comb them and comb them. When I chopped them off
—because he was getting big and I couldn't let him go on forever
looking like a girl—I wrapped them up and sent them to my
husband. He was in Zakynthos then. The time of the earthquakes,
when they lost everything, he wrote me that of all he lost, it was
those blond curls I'd sent him he regretted most. . . ."

We have toiled for the nation's independence, nor did we begrudge
our last penny. But at least that we might see our nation prosper. . . .
'Tis this incenses us! . . . 'Tis this crushes us! . . . To see you slaves,
when with our very teeth we sundered your yoke. . . .
                                                    —*Thanos Vlekas*

• Village outside Athens.
    "Did you ask after us in the street?" the aging mother demands,
all in a jitter.
    "No," I assure her.
    "We're scared out of our wits," says her daughter. "We still live
in bondage."
    Her aged father's in bed asleep and stays that way all the time
I'm there. He used to be a butcher and managed to make a little
money. But since retiring he's gone downhill. They won't let him
out by himself after dark. He gets muddled, loses his way, and is
always being brought home by other people. The family can boast
one son killed, one in prison, and an admiral for an uncle. His
was the voice over the radio during the occupation that drove his
nephews to take to the hills. But now he won't lift a finger to help
the captive.
    "My younger brother," says the daughter, "was tortured to death.
He was having a good time in the village café when they beat
him and kicked him all the way down to the police station. He
was only twenty. A neighbor living next door to the police station
came around and told me she didn't get a wink of sleep all night
because of the screams from the cellar. I went around to make
inquiries. 'We never touched him,' they said. We couldn't get him
out. But a friend of his, a Yank from the airfield, pulled it off.

Not long after that he died. Forty days after the arrest my big brother came out of hiding to show up at the funeral. The entire security brigade descended on the church to catch him. But we—the family, that is—shielded him with our backs. All made a ring around him. They didn't catch him that day. Caught up with him later. When they tried him at Halkis and his lawyer asked the prosecution witness to point him out from all the accused, the false witness didn't know and picked the wrong man."

"In those days the courts came down pretty hard," adds the girl's fiancé, also present. "God wasn't in it."

The mother leaves us for a few minutes and goes upstairs. She comes down with a framed picture, a photo of her dead son, wrapped in faded newspaper. She unfolds it with great care, guiltily, closing the door.

"We used to keep it hidden away in the trunk. Never took it out," she says. "But now, with our son-in-law, we're a little more sure of ourselves."

The photograph shows the young fellow dead but bandoleered, though on him the bandoleers lack any air of brutality. They're for effect, rather, like the sashes adorning village beauty queens, or like the cowboy outfits kids today have their picture taken in. His face looks pure and innocent, his glance as if a girl were eying him. No trace of what the phrase "bandoleered rebel" usually conjures up in our minds, with, more often than not, a beard enhancing his ferocity. An idealized figure, as in a poem by Cavafy.

"If he'd acted otherwise, you'd have had something to worry about," says the future son-in-law to the old lady. "What he did was his sacred duty to his country."

"They banished me to Chios," says the daughter, "on account of my brother. It's a miracle we're alive!"

"Truth is, others were to blame," says her fiancé.

"Some of the fellows from the village football team went off to see him in Crete. At the time he was arrested they were just little kids, always in and out of our mulberry bushes. 'It's a crime to keep a good guy like Nikos in there,' they said when they got back. He kissed them all and said, 'This kiss for you is a kiss for the village, a kiss for all Greece.' "

"Born poor, die poor," said the assessor.

"Injustice howls to the third heaven," old Lachanopoulos cried.

"Who shall tend my beasts? I had a son of age. . . . I am an old man, lame and helpless. . . ."

"You all howl at once like a pack of dogs in the pen," the assessor rebuked them.

"Of course," retorted Assimina. " 'Tis not your child they steal, and thus to you our wailing seems of no account. Are we to be slaughtered yet not speak out? What manner of man is that?"

—*Thanos Vlekas*

• Ano Daphni. Sunday afternoon.

. . . Here we are, listeners, in the twenty-second minute of the first half, and the score in the Olympiakos-Panathenaïkos match stands level at nothing to nothing. Right now the ball is at the feet of Gregoriades. . . .

A communal courtyard. In one of its cells, with a sheet for a door, lives the old lady. A couple of her neighbors have the soccer game blaring full strength from the radio. The old lady's all on her own. Ugly, with a dulcet voice.

"Can't read or write," she says. "Lord Jesus above come to our aid! Born and bred in Santorini, I was. My husband starved to death in '42. Sure, he was a family man, brought us our daily bread. I got my daughter placed in service; she'd bring me a morsel. My son, he'd race around here, there, and everywhere for the sake of a crust. I'm just a wretched old hag. . . .

"He was sixteen years old when he went inside," she continues. "What in the world could he know about it? He was meek as a virgin, in the flower of his youth. He fell in with a bunch of crooks; they told him he could be eating with a silver spoon. It's silver spoons we've been eating with for eighteen years now. Little fish'll never eat the big one. . . . When Zakynthos jail fell down, he was half swallowed up in the rubble. He wrote me, 'It was your prayers saved me, Mom, and I was spared.'

"A kindhearted Christian lady took pity on me and lodged me in this little room. She pays my rent. Only the bed's my own. I was counting on the boy to take care of me. Four brothers, I had, but they're all dead. And a sister confined to her bed back home. Back home we knew nothing about commies and the like. 'Sign, Christos,' I wrote him. 'I'll be out when the time comes, Mother,' he told me. My daughter's married, got a daughter of her own, eighteen years old. They all live together, husband and all, in the one room. . . . My son's no murderer. He just trotted around wherever they told him. The judge had no cause to lock him up for twenty years. They've got him washing dishes in the prison cookhouse. Sure, how many innocent lads are in there for nothing? Lord Jesus Christ! O Lord Jesus!

"They beat him up so bad he was spitting blood. To make him swear to what he saw. What could he see, now, a boy of sixteen? What would he know about it? A bunch of crooks . . . Silver spoons . . . Eighteen years now since I've seen him—I never go out, can't walk. 'Don't cry, Mom,' he writes me. 'Tell yourself I'm in America. Think what it's like for other mothers who've lost their sons for good. Never fear, you'll be seeing me one day. . . .' There's a woman goes back and forth between here and the prison. 'Any message for your boy Christos?' she asks me. What's there to say but I'm waiting for him? . . . The Dear Lord Jesus help us!"

We leave. Sunday afternoon, assassinated by so many soccer games, so many lottery coupons, so many weddings. Everywhere huge limousines beribboned in white and bearing off brides and grooms. Lines outside the photographers'. A hood in the refugee quarter strolls arm in arm with a lady tourist. Crowds pour out of the stadiums in a surging tempestuous rush, obstructing the stream of taxis whisking off the newlyweds to their first night of marriage. Sunday afternoon. Life has not come to a standstill, as it has in the homes we've seen. A policeman shouting with a civilian . . . No, it's not what I first assumed, under the influence of the stories I've just heard. Quite simply, one supports Olympiakos and the other Panathenaikos. . . . Dusk.

This inquiry could have been taken further, into more homes, with little to add in the way of variety. The stories vary only in detail. One home might contain more prison handwork, another less. One absentee doing life, another twenty years. One under Category A, for the well-to-do and educated prisoners; another under Category B, for the poor and ignorant. "You haven't written me yet whether sowing's finished or how the olives are going on," writes one prisoner. "You're eighteen years old now," writes another on his son's birthday. "Health and long life I wish you. I wish you many years and happy, and steady progress in your schooling, too. Eighteen years of life for you. Seventeen years of jail for me. . . . Let us cross the threshold of your eighteenth year with hope, let us look to the future with optimism." One minister demands a declaration of recantation; another, a letter to the newspapers from the prisoner recognizing the present government. Only in one home did we find a difference: the mother, who was laying out camomile on the floor to dry, showed much greater anxiety than the others we met. The reason was that her forty-seven-year-old son had been released a few days ago. She was scared we'd come to investigate. "They're keeping tabs on him," she told us. "Where he goes, who he sees."

On her lined face could be read all the signs of anguish. Her son was away. She'd packed him off to her uncle's, in Haïdari, "to take the air." Vicious circle.

Thanos Vlekas, by Pavlos Kalligas, is the first modern Greek novel. Published in Pandora in the middle of the last century, it faithfully portrays the "Little Greece" of Otto. . . .

If I've referred to it so frequently within the space of this inquiry, it's not so much that I wish to pay due tribute to its author as that I see no difference between Otto's "Little Greece" and Paul's "Great Greece" of today.

Its painful topicality and contemporaneity stem from the fact that "the newly born Nation and amorphous society" it describes unfortunately persist to the present day. Like it or not, despite all outward appearance to the contrary, we are, at least from the point of view of progress, in the selfsame situation we found ourselves in over 100 years ago, at the time this novel was written.

"The creative imagination investing a symbol or type," writes critic Tsokopoulos, referring to *Thanos Vlekas*, "is here put to little use. The craftsman produced photographs, and indeed with a candid camera. Art took no trouble to retouch."

This is lucky, for we stand in great need of such documents, unerring barometers of our static society.

Newly Released

What does one imagine when one reads in the papers that "another 420 political prisoners have been released" or "there are now 120 in our prisons" or "many of the political prisoners find it impossible to return to their villages" or "the government ought to aid the newly released"? What lies concealed behind the label "political prisoner"? Up to now, we've known only political leaders and political economists. We now find joining us on the open plains of our so-called freedom so-called political prisoners. But what in fact do they represent? Is it a question of men who, like Rip Van Winkle, having slumbered for years and years, suddenly awake to a world strange and unfamiliar? Is it a question of anarchic elements whose illicit activities will undermine the foundation of society? Or is it more a question of martyrs who've escaped the lions, like those first Christians uneaten by the gorged beasts sprawled on the lush grass of the Roman arena digesting their dinner; the lucky or unluckiest, to whom the emperor showed mercy, allowing them to emerge with a feeling of guilt for surviving, yet also without a qualm since they faltered not in the face of the direst ordeal? And if so, what are the problems they face? What do they think of today, of our today and their today? What do they think of all they've seen and suffered and borne witness to? How might they envisage the future? All this prompted me with the notion of going and getting to know them up close, at home, among their families so long deprived of them, so long gnawing black bread and bitter sun. So to the same homes I'd once visited to harken to the sorrow of mother, wife, or child, I now returned to harken to the men themselves. The homes are the same as last year's, in the same slum neighborhoods that will stay the same for years, for whole decades—refugee ghettoes unassimilated by the body of society, withered branches unnourished by the sap of the national trunk, like cart tracks intersecting the national highway, as incongruous as the announcer with the facts he is announcing.

• Antiquity and mythology as a street plan for the squalidest of slums. An interesting study for Neo-Hellenists. "BUILDING PLOT FOR SALE. CINEMA COMING SOON." "Mechanics, Plumbers, Do-It-Yourself Handymen, It Pays You to Pay Us a Call." "Wide Range of Sanitary Appliances." "Incredibly Easy Payments at Common Market Prices." "*SuperSlumb*er Mattresses and Bedding." "Original Molded Glassware." "Parishioners, Your Monthly Subscription Will Greatly Aid the Completion of Your Church."

The old man just out of jail isn't home. His son is sorting out his papers to leave for Germany. Not that he has no job here, but since his father's been back, he hasn't felt right. Over the last twenty years he'd grown used to living alone with his mother here in this hovel. Just the two of them. Now they're three, he doesn't exactly feel he belongs. A drama unfolding in darkness. Perhaps deeper than subconscious, even. He's a cobbler by trade. He writes. Hands me a scenario, *The Stalactite Dwellers*, inspired by an ancient legend about the caves of Mani. Wants me to read it, wants my opinion. He showed it to the actor Alexandakis when *Dream Suburb* was being shot at nearby Asyrmatos. Theodorakis, too, had seemed willing to help. Now both are otherwise engaged. A sensitive boy who hides his feelings. The return of his father forever weeping on his aged wife's shoulder fills no gap. Merely opens up a new one. The human body now occupies a precise, visible space. For twenty years he'd learned to live with his absence. So he'd made the decision to leave with a friend of his for Germany.

• Hippothontides Street. "Frozen Fish, Deep Freeze. Regular Deliveries. Gurnard, Mullet." Tiny Tobacconist's. Evergreen Fruiterer's. Concord Cobbler's. Plato Garage. "DIVERSE PREMISES TO LET." "Wheaten Loaves, Country Style."

I found him in the middle of moving. He was about to lift a heavy wardrobe unaided, clean forgetting his ruptured spinal disc. The lady next door tells me he can't stay on his feet for more than half an hour at a time without his stick. But he keeps at it. He won't give in. He does any and every job a hale and healthy husband would do. The new home where I find him—the rent's cheaper—consists all in all of two rooms, cement dank, on the ground floor, like two adjoining prison cells. He seats himself on the divan. At first we're alone. Then, one by one, we're joined by all the neighbors.

"I've had this complaint," he tells me, "since the Italians tortured me in Lysicratus Street. The *milizia* really wrecked my back. Write down my ailments: duodenal ulcer, an old injury to the iris of my left eye—from beatings at security headquarters—chronic inflammation of the ear, rheumatoid arthritis all over my body. Sometimes catches me in the arm, sometimes the leg. Now we're done with that, where shall I start? Quite a mess. Anyway there's one thing special about my case: I was invalided out three times as incurable. Twice in 1958 and once in 1960. That was when I got married and my boy was born. The kid holding the placard in the pictures in the papers: GIVE ME BACK MY FATHER. Last eighteen days since I come out, I've had a real flood of welcomes home and good wishes. I couldn't sleep but an hour or two. Now I'm looking for a job. It'll have to be a job where I'm not on my feet all day long. Best thing'd be janitoring, but I ain't got the money. Anyway, whatever job it is, I won't do nothing against my conscience. I'd die first, let 'em squeeze the blood outa me drop by drop, but I won't go against my conscience."

He coughs. In the next room the neighbors are riveted with admiration.

"Before the war," he resumes, "I was a clerk at the Ministry of Health and Social Welfare. After the war I worked again for a spell. Just when I thought it was all over, they chucked me in the death cell. Since then I been living on borrowed time. With the retrial I was reprieved and got life. But from then on I been plagued with the feeling it was by some error I was still alive. That I'm an extra ration, not the ration itself. All those years staring death in the face, from the day they condemned me with one voice to death to the day they reprieved me, how else was I supposed to feel? Death is unbearable anyway. But when there's a way out, then it's really more than you can take. For us, the way out was the declaration. So what with not signing it all them years, don't that mean we truly did believe our sacrifice served some greater purpose? At heart we're the truly liberated ones. The unfettered. The indomitable. Wrecks now. So what! I was only a boy when I went inside. Push a button and I'd jump up like a jack-in-the-box. Now . . . But our ideals we keep close in our souls."

He keeps coughing.

"Where do you start, where do you finish? A mess all right. Life in jail was nothing but torment. But we don't hate anybody. The man who murdered my mother in her bed, he has my full pardon. We bear no grudges. We expected after the liberation to do our bit toward rebuilding the country. But they foisted the civil war on us. Yet all them years we held the flame aloft between our very teeth. I'm a contender for the people and proud of it.

"What did we go through? What can you say about it now? All I can tell you is, when you see films like *The Man in the Iron Mask* and such, that's nothing compared to what we suffered.

"Now me and the wife, we're like a pair of lovebirds, facing all life's hardships with songs and laughter. We may not have a scrap to eat, but nothing wipes the song from our lips. When we left the other place everyone was in tears. They'd grown so used to our singing! My wife, write this down, she's a credit to her sex. And it's my firm belief that today it takes a new type of man and woman to stand up effectively to the onslaught of electricity and Americanocracy on all fronts. We're a couple without anguish. The couple of the future."

I ask him if he's ever bothered by the security police, and he replies, "No, but someone gave me the wink there's a security tail

on me. So I came right out and told him my movements are
quite normal and straightforward."

• Saint Michael's bus stop. Waiting for the Kato Petralona bus.
An old man hawking strings of figs by the decorative-tiles works.
An old woman hawking ring doughnuts in between the wheels
of the trucks and three-wheelers bunched up at the red light,
which is always slow changing to green. Above the mass of low
houses the specter of the Acropolis hovers over the eternal squalor.
A huge American limousine glides between the old woman's
doughnuts and the old man's figs.

He's been whitewashing the house for Easter, so it's a while
before he comes out. Sitting in the room, his wife, her parents, and
a neighbor who's given birth to triplets. Only his daughter is
missing, the daughter he left a nine-day-old baby and found an
eighteen-year-old girl. Soon he, too, appears, first having cleaned
himself up. From the sideboard he produces an album, like a
scrapbook, full of handwritten poems wreathed with designs. "No
poet," it says on the first page, "wrote these poems. A father wrote
them for his child. I wrote them for you, my precious little daughter." With reverence I leaf through the album, all present amazed
at my attaching such importance to it. Hurriedly I jot down two
of the poems in my notebook:

ANEMONE

My child of nine,
alone you have grown
unkissed and uncaressed
in your father's empty arms,
as in our garden blooms
a lone anemone.

LIKE TO MY SECRET JOY

Winter in our garden
furtively burgeoned,

like to our secret hopes,
and spoke of spring,
the pansy velvet,
the snow-white stock,
carnation scarlet,
ere snows had thawed.
Two or three flowers
that sunless bloomed,
like to my secret joy,
you would I send.

"She's a full-grown young lady now," he says. "I go to give her a kiss, she backs off. I haven't been a father to her since she was a baby. Missed her growing up year by year. . . ."

Then, changing the subject, he tells me that as one of the prisoners released by judicial decree he has to report once a fortnight to security headquarters. And to go see his sister who lives in Thebes he has to get permission from security, then report to the Thebes Police Department.

"But the most pressing problem's still money. What kind of resources can we embark with on our conquest of the world? We go to the Red Cross for help during our first few months of freedom. All we can expect coming out of prison is 150 drachs apiece sent by an American minister from Kentucky. No other assistance whatsoever."

The course of the conversation changes. One by one the faces before me fade. The walls change color, darken, to black. The memory floods back like a childhood nightmare. I'm absorbed with him in his account of the prison camp on Yaros. First night. Just arrived. The fires under the line of cauldrons light up the harsh craggy slope where 5,000 exiles wait with their mess tins ready to receive a ladleful of worm-eaten beans. The cauldrons belch smoke into the twilight like the funnels of ocean liners. His turn. As he draws near the cauldron the stench grabs his nostrils and he passes out. A bamboo cane brings him round, biting into his back; unfamiliar with camp regulations, he still has his cap on.

The black beans stink. He gulps them down with water. Still, he can't swallow them. Someone gropes through the darkness to ask him for them. He dips into the parcel he has with him for something to eat. Bread, canned or bottled food, the very crumbs are shared among all the old convicts in the tent. . . . Then Corfu. Summertime. Rotting in the sweltering dormitories. The order given to lock all cell doors because six prisoners have escaped. Building human pyramids to reach the windows, they yell out their complaints about the goings on to the people of Corfu. To drown the voice of protest, army megaphones are brought in. But their voices outshout the megaphones and march music. As a last vengeful resort, the guards wreck the flower beds along every spoke of the prison, one cyclamen alone surviving the insane vandalism, hidden under a sheet hung from the window. This cyclamen becomes the prisoners' last hope. Doctor Siganos, with his passion for flowers, waters it surreptitiously from the prison buttresses, until one day the sheet was blown aside by a stiff breeze to reveal the now good-sized flower. Whereupon the guards swooped in rabid frenzy and tore it up by the roots. "Back, you Turks!" howled the doctor. "Back!"

The colors fade. The faces of the relatives swim back into the room. Outside it's almost dusk. Easter draws nigh.

"We'll roast a rat or two on the spit," says his father-in-law.

On the table a miniature ship and a lamp, prison handwork, tattoos embroidered on the skin of sea dogs and jailbirds.

• The man I want to see isn't home at this hour. He's out all day looking for a job, his sister tells me. He was a medical student when they put him in prison, and he has acquired vast medical experience there. But the wherewithal for taking his degree is now lacking. Besides, he'd prefer to work, to lighten his family's financial burden. All he requires is a job as assistant in some pharmaceutical firm where he'd at least enjoy the illusion of being in his element. Though this is something of a drawback, because the words "political prisoner" alone are enough to arouse that faint flicker of mistrust in any employer.

"How did you find him after so many years?" I ask his sister on the doorstep, despite her every plea to come inside and wait.

"He's turned so sensitive," she tells me. "Gets upset over nothing. Slightest thing has him in tears. Whatever you say to him, he cries. The first few nights he couldn't sleep. Couldn't even walk. He'd say, 'I walk like I've been drinking.' And at first he'd speak very low. He kept thinking they'd hear him, like inside. 'Speak up! Speak up!' we'd yell at him. He's settled down now. But our old dad's suddenly aged since he got out. All the excitement's worn him out. . . . I'm sorry to say there's no regular time he gets back. Sometimes in the afternoon, sometimes not. Come back whenever you like. I'll tell him."

• A café near the bridge. A nonsmoking teetotaler sporting a new overcoat, a present from his son-in-law, and an almost unnatural freshness of face. Nineteen years inside. He insists on paying for my coffee.

"During the holiday period," he tells me, "there was a whole rush of releases. Christmas Eve, thirty released. New Year's Eve, another forty. Epiphany, I come out along with forty-two others. . . . New Year's Eve I was at work in the prison cookhouse. Around seven, half past, one of the regular convicts—he used to mix with the visitors—come and told me a telegram had arrived at the warden's office saying I was to be released. Then a guard comes and tells me the warden wants to see me. So off I go, and he congratulates me and hands me my release card. The fellows were overjoyed. It was only then I really got to believe after nineteen years I was actually gonna be released.

"In fact, that evening I lost all appetite. Began to wonder what'd happen now, how would I face my folks. I'd lost my cool, as they say. Next day, New Year's, my mother come to Aegina. Luck would have it she arrived the minute the forty released on New Year's Day were coming out, and she starts asking, 'Ain't Yiannis with you?' You see, the procedure takes seven to eight days from when the minister signs the decree to the actual release. One time it used to take two weeks. Afterward, when I came out to see my mother, she confirmed all the efforts, for everybody, had turned up trumps. Then we starts talking over how the two of us were to manage.

"When visiting time was over, she went off, and I started getting my things together. What books should I take with me, what clothes, and what about my bed? Each man had his own camp bed because what with being shunted around from one prison to another, we never knew what sort of state the next place'd be in. So's not to have to sleep on bare cement and risk catching pleurisy, we'd take our own beds with us.

"Epiphany, it was, when our turn came. Forty-two of us, biggest batch yet. Lot of us wept to be leaving the others behind. No tears from them. On the contrary, they rejoiced at our farewell. For us it was agony the other lads weren't coming out, too. Handshakes, messages, hugs, and kisses were the order of the day. And on that great day we even forgave the warders who'd bullied us and put us through all kinds of pain and torture.

"We didn't make the pilgrimage to Tourlos like the previous batch. Tourlos is an isolated beacon on Aegina. Germans had coastal gun emplacements there. Then it came to be a place of execution. They let us out at that hour of the day, between four and five in the afternoon just so we couldn't go. So we all made our way to Aegina Cemetery. It was dusk on a wet afternoon. First, sixteen executed were buried there in mass graves, and later, the others, executed in 1948. You might take note of the fact that the graves are all abandoned. Only a couple of crosses bear the names of two friends of mine. One of us said a few words, another recited a poem by the executed poet Costas Yiannopoulos. It began, 'I and my sister'—maybe you know it, a poem he wrote in the death cell on the eve of execution. We observed a minute's silence, then left. We loaded our few things into one-horse buggies and a big taxicab and went down to the harbor. People on the jetty, when they heard we were political prisoners just released, straight away showed great sympathy. We tested our legs on the street, and it seemed strange to be able to walk around freely. The life of routine, life ruled by the bell, as we say, was at long last over. Now we were free to walk, and not only on the cross of the prison yard.

"We reached Piraeus on the boat. There we split up. Fellows from the country went to stay with relatives or at hotels. I went to my married sister's.

"That first night I slept in the same room as my mother. What struck me most was the light being off. For all of nineteen years we'd gotten used to sleeping every night with the light glaring over our heads.

"Next day was Saint John's and the whole family set off for the home of some friends who were giving a party. There were lots of people. I sat in a corner and watched them having a whale of a time, with wine and fancy tidbits to nibble on, things I'd forgotten about. I was afraid to say a word. Everything seemed so strange, so totally novel.

"In the days that followed, I had to have somebody with me even to go buy a comb. Then I went to the police station to get my identity card. I took along my release card, the ministry decree, and the certificate from Athens City Hall. The chief of police asked me whether I had papers, meaning had I signed the declaration of recantation. When I told him I hadn't, he said okay and ordered the issue of my identity card, just like any other citizen.

"Prison life was a sort of reflection of political life on the outside, and we caught the backlash of every situation all the harder, the purpose of every prison being to provide them with a bogeyman for folks outside. Take General Plastiras—under him things slacked off in jail. With Papagos' bunch they tightened up again. The period of executions was followed by a period of pressure for the declaration. The guards even got to the point, out there on the cross—that crossroads inside the prison separating the various blocks—of tossing out a rope, symboliclike, to see who'd rise to the bait. Those who bit and got their release never came back to our dormitories to collect their things. They sent guards. But there were others man enough to own up. 'Boys,' they'd say, 'we've had a bellyful. We want out.' That we could understand.

"You asked me which prisons were worst. For buildings, the worst were Corfu, Kefallinia, Lefkada, and Yaros. For administration, Corfu, Itzedin, and Kefallinia. But at Aegina, too, they certainly took care of us! Last two campaigns against us took place in July 1960 and June 1962. Guards raided our dormitories—with cops down on the cross—and confiscated everything: photos, books, even our stamps. Chucked out our clothes and split us up into haves and have-nots, educated and ignorant. Closed down our workshops—cobbler's, office, tailor shop, even our sick bay, as there were doctors and nurses among us—then brought in microphones and started haranguing us. Some big noise from the Ministry of Justice come and made another speech about the declaration. Seventeen years we done for that very reason. Did he think he was gonna change our minds now? He crawled off with his tail between his legs. With letters to the press we managed to put a stop to the microphones and propaganda. The minister showed up, but all he authorized was the reopening of the canteen. Oh, but I do beg your pardon. I must be going. I'm a long way from home and they'll be expecting me for dinner."

Strolling down the street, he bumps into another newly released prisoner. "Meet my wife," says the latter. The man at my side seems not to have heard. "My wife," the other man repeats. I watch him turn, shake her hand, and say, "Pleased to meet you," careful not to look her in the face.

• A tailor's shop in Kato Patissia. Five people altogether. Three newly released prisoners, tailors by trade, the kindhearted storekeeper who gave them jobs, and a friend just passing, also newly released.

The whole time we're talking they don't stop working for a second, cutting and sewing material, wadding, machine-stitching linings, ironing—in this cramped, prisonlike cell. Stabbed in the back by the draught from the open window and with no room to shift position, I shut the window, and soon the tiny room fogs up with smoke.

"The prison drama's all over. Now for Act One of the new drama, the struggle for a living," says the tall counter tenor with big expressive hands, like the tailor in the Italian movie *The Bespoke Overcoat.*

"A three-act drama," adds the visitor. "One: finding a job. Two: getting identity cards. Three: dodging the draft."

"The draft?"

"That's right, the draft. A lot of us who've just come out never done our national service. When our age-groups got called up, we were in jail. Ministry issued a series of extensions for buying your way out, but last one expired the end of December 1963. So those of us released after New Year's could be summoned to the service of our country, or, worse, declared draft dodgers—ain't that what they call 'em?—court-martialed, and locked up again. In our position we've learned to fear the worst."

"They put you out through one door and pull you back in through the other," says the storekeeper, with the needle between his lips.

"They oughta give us a further extension, whether or not we can find the 4,500 drachs to buy our way out."

"Yessiree," says the boss, stitching the seam of a jacket. "You need a tidy sum for military expenses. On top of that, keep moaning about being out of work and they'll tell you, 'We'll make a soldier of you so your mess tin'll always be full.' Real charitable of 'em."

"You see," the visitor throws back over his shoulder from the doorway, "nineteen years inside and now two years in the army is just too much, really, especially in our condition. . . ."

"Ostracized from the world for nineteen years," someone else picks up the thread of the sentence as their friend leaves, closing the door behind him, "how else could we feel but like fish out of water? In prison, naturally enough, we lived in a world of our own making, but whatever we did with it, it couldn't possibly be anything like the real world we're having to cope with now."

"Prison life had a certain continuity," says the counter tenor with the expressive hands. "Our little society was molded differently. What's struck us coming out is the anguish most people seem to be suffering. A maggot slowly gnawing into us as well."

"A needle's all we got to our name. I can't live on what I earn, can't even afford an evening out at a club or squander fifty drachs after spending twenty years of my life behind bars. I've gone to the movies just once in the two months I've been out."

"We're guys who need a job, guys just starting out in life, like we'd have been starting out twenty years ago."

"We certainly don't want to live at anyone else's expense. All we want is to work. We're okay. A goodhearted fella come along and took us into his shop. But what about the others? A batch of 450 are shortly due out. What're all those fellas gonna do?"

"It's quite a struggle for us to get back into the swim. Of course, in prison we were roughly aware of what was going on outside; we pieced things together. But once outside it's very hard to keep up. We can't say if we'll ever be able to properly."

"When I got out I went home to my village. I was really impressed by the reception they gave me. Relatives and friends 'occupied' the whole house. People even came to see me though there was blood between us. Only the village priest wasn't there to greet me, though there's never been anything personal between him and me. Has 'Love one another' turned to 'Hate everyone' over the years? Sure, I was expecting the folks back home in the village to be pleased at my release. But I never expected them to be that pleased."

"My place became a shrine for the populace."

"Everyone greeted us with open arms."

"Such a warm welcome everybody gave us. Even the opposition were openly moved and said how much they regretted not being able to speed up the process of getting us back in their midst. My first cousin, who's right wing, she swooned with joy the minute she set eyes on me."

"What we're saying is the wounds have healed in the hearts of the people. It's only the actual government, the state, that for the time being still looks askance at us and keeps out of sight. They just send around a couple of cops, I imagine, to find out where we are and what we're up to. A plain-clothes man called at my father-in-law's. Claimed he was a grocer and I owed him 300 drachs."

"One come to my sister's place, where I'm staying. It's no more than a hovel. You see, they're trying to give the people who shelter us the idea they're running some kind of risk."

"What about the actual village? How did you find things there?" I ask.

"My village was completely destroyed in the quakes. My mother and father've since died. I was a complete stranger to my sister's new house. Everything gave me a feeling of bitterness and sorrow."

"Before the war my village had a population of 450. Now there's just 160. The primary school used to take 96 pupils. Today, 13. The others have all gone. Athens, Canada, Argentina, Brazil. Complete and utter decimation. Revenue's dropped. Wine produce, oranges and lemons, all slackened off. Figs disappeared. Only olive oil's still going strong. In fact, output's on the increase."

"Even the countryside seemed altered. Most of the villagers, I didn't recognize. I left 'em boys and girls and found 'em full-grown men and women."

"That first night coming up from Piraeus to Athens all I could see was a river of lights. I was overwhelmed by the traffic, all the cars, the rhythm of life we'd only heard the sound of before. Only way you could imagine the world as it is today is in a dream."

"Right from the first, it struck me all the bouzouki music they play on the radio and everybody sings. Before the war you only heard bouzouki in the hashish dens. And for all they've refined it since those days, it still sounds pessimistic. Why not make the clarinet our national instrument? The clarinet's got spirit. It offends my ears to listen to the radio. Greeks are just imitating foreigners. They've cut themselves off from the national trunk; we've forgotten our popular traditions, the roots. I found my niece tuning the radio to all the bouzouki programs. I'm gradually trying to give her a taste for classical music. Beethoven. I confiscate the cheap magazines she buys and give her serious books to read. It takes time, but her outlook's slowly changing."

"It's our dream that someday history'll be written as it really happened, and we'll take our rightful place."

Four

FLC

Late as usual, the subaltern strolled in, flicking his cap off with a bored "Good morning."

"CO been after me?" he asked.

"No," said Apostolis.

The sun hadn't yet topped the Great Britain building opposite. Chambermaids were dusting balconies and wiping down windows. Through a half-drawn curtain a young female figure could be glimpsed flitting to and fro in a pink petticoat. Apostolis' gaze alternated between her and the policeman in the street below chasing away a young doughnut vendor. Early-morning pedestrians jockeyed unconcerned with early-season tourists. The woman opposite soon disappeared into the bathroom, and the doughnut boy vanished among the columns of the arcade, which also housed an underground garage.

Apostolis turned his gaze on the common room, where the lamp was still ablaze. The subaltern had opened a book and was reading. What did he care? With a Central Market butcher for a father, he could get meat two drachs cheaper for his CO, the center commandant, and bones gratis for the CO's dog. Apostolis went to fetch them every morning at eleven. At three he fetched them again, this time packed in the CO's briefcase, and was first one out, to reserve him a seat on the Papagos bus at the Syntagma Square terminal. The CO would arrive shortly after, escorted by his adjutant. The soldier surrendered the briefcase, saluted—*"Bon appétit"*—and was dismissed. . . . Hence the subaltern lost no sleep over punctuality.

The bell sounded first break, and Albanian accents made the first sortie into the common room. Mr. Donias' gross mustache brought with it yet deeper shades. By contrast, beaming as usual, in trotted Lunik, namely Mr. Vletos. Next, the Russian quartet rumbled in. With heavy gait and listing rearward, as if plodding through a boggy field in his army boots, Mr. Patsakov, czarist-cavalry veteran and now retired armored-corps officer, tête-à-tête with Mrs. Ilyushkaya while endeavoring to light his pipe, like a leftover cannon from a bombed-out tank. *"Niet do lexik,"* retorted the ample Russian matron, who called her officer-pupils "my little ones, my darlings" as she drooled with tenderness. While the English, who stood out from the defectors by not ganging up, strolled in one by one to occupy vacant chairs without so much as a word. The common room became once more the familiar smoke-filled menagerie.

Apostolis listened. Phonemes bombarded his ears. He watched the bald head, winged with ears like deciduous leaves in fall, of retired Brigadier Ilirov, who flared up when addressed by name, though when Apostolis called him "Brigadier, sir" instantly responded, "What is it, my boy?"; watched him hopping about like a frog in search of somewhere to prop his briefcase and then, relieved of this encumbrance, gesticulating for added panache in front of Mrs. Tatianova's prodigious bosom, who always arrived moody in the mornings, sat in her chair in silence, and left when classes were over with an *"au revoir, à demain"*; watched the subaltern opposite still reading with his hands clamped over his ears; watched Mr. Donias, who passed out his king-size filters to the Albanians, and spread open in front of him the grade books in which he had to list the grades and figure the averages, ruled out with draftsmanlike zeal by the CO himself, lines, rails, railway tracks no train ever rode over. And once more Apostolis fell to counting the minutes before the bell sounded the end of break, just as he counted the days before discharge, end of the year at this Foreign Language Center which he was thoroughly sick of, from grades and grade books down to the CO's theories on the Jewish conspiracy, the seed of Abraham, and the reconstitution of the State of Israel; as sick of being personally responsible for the registered stock and equipment of the center, earphones, clinometers, amplifiers, cymometers, verniers, oscillators, potentiometers, as of the adjutant's theories on women and big-business projects for building houses out of demolition materials from the Brussels Exhibition. And here he was, surrounded by the wild beasts whining and groaning in their cramped cage, when a male hand stroked his face, while almost on the stroke came the voice, "Shave with the Remington today?"

He recoiled. To no man did he permit such undue familiarity. His eyes met Mr. Chliveros, tutor of "correct pronunciation, grammatical accuracy, and syntactical coherence in conversation from the good book *Beginning Lessons in English*," whose dearest wish for weeks now had been to buy an electric razor and who, with no idea which brand to choose, went around asking everybody, craving counsel everywhere.

"Yes," Apostolis replied, getting up, crossing to the window, and opening it to let the smoke out; though because Mrs. Linou, tutor in military literature, felt chilly, he was soon obliged to close it again.

"Have much of a job getting a shave like that?" Mr. Chliveros now inquired, minutely scrutinizing every pore to see if the Remington hadn't perchance left an odd bristle here and there.

"Not at all," Apostolis assured him, giving his cheek a second rub, not so much for confirmation of a clean shave as to wipe off the dirty feel left by the alien caress, while through the closed window he watched a blond tripping past the ETAM shop front.

"So you'd advise me to plump for the Remington as against the Browning?"

"That's my advice," Apostolis said, his eyes glued to the girl, who now stood gaping in the shopwindow.

"But my whiskers are coarser than yours. The blades of the Remington mightn't shave them so close, clean as a whistle, you know. . . ."

"All depends, old chap," Apostolis rejoined as his eyes followed the girl in her clinging outfit swinging her hams down the arcade, to disappear among its columns, whence he saw the spongeseller emerge, girt with a holster of white and coffee-colored sponges, to cross the street unperturbed by traffic hurtling around the corner at breakneck speed. I envy you, poor spongeseller, he thought, gliding along in your cloud immune and invulnerable to the shafts of the metropolis.

He turned his gaze back on the common room—why the sudden urge to call it "common grave"?—and, finding Mr. Chliveros poised to carry on the conversation, decided to pass the new examination timetable among the tutors; on CO's orders they all had to sign it, as having "received notice thereof." First he approached the Albanian brigade huddled beneath the portrait of Paul and Frederika.

"What do you need us to sign now?" asked Mr. Donias, in his pin-striped suit, seemingly, by height and confidential position in one of the ministries, their leader.

"It's the examination timetable," said Apostolis.

"*Fert yiler*," snatching it from his hands to lean on the table and read it. Craning over him they all produced pads and jotted down dates and times. Only Lunik couldn't see. Apostolis waited to one side.

"Where do we sign?"

"Under 'Received and Noted.' "

At that moment the coffee vendor stole into the common room with a very sweet coffee for Mrs. Linou and a jam tart for Mr. Chliveros. He was making a brave bid for invisibility, but the white apron, despite its grime, betrayed him. Strictly for reasons of security, the adjutant, second in command of the center, had barred him from the classrooms. During breaks his pitch was restricted to the landing outside the entrance to the corridor. But Babis the coffee vendor knew well enough that if he didn't shove his wares under his customers' noses he'd have iced coffee in his cups and yellow salami between stale bread. So he took care to keep in with the CO—giving him coffee half-price and his habitual one-o'clock cognac with sugar gratis—risking lightning raids into the classrooms, snatching orders from the very air. Though all depended on the two duty orderlies in the orderly room and the touchy nerves of the adjutant himself. Whenever it was time to pay, they fell out. They claimed he padded the bills, he claimed he marked down everything on the cuff, and the adjutant always raved, "Set foot in the center again and I'll confiscate your coffees!" Then he'd forget, and when they met in the corridor he said not a word. Which seemed to be the state of their relations today as he brought in the very sweet coffee for Mrs. Linou and the jam tart for Mr. Chliveros.

Lunik was last to squiggle his initials. Apostolis picked up the sheet and crossed to the Russian party, clustered in the opposite corner under the icon of Christ Crucified. Mrs. Tatianova was putting on her overcoat with the gallant aid of retired Pithe-canthropus, Brigadier Ilirov, on tiptoe. She was about to leave with an *"au revoir, à demain,"* when Apostolis caught her at the door with a *"Madame."*

"Qu'est-ce que c'est?"

"Signez le programme, s'il vous plaît."

"But I signed it yesterday."

"Yesterday's is canceled."

"Have you a spare copy for me?" asked Mr. Patsakov, blowing out pipe smoke.

"No more copies. You sign this one."

"Very well, next break," he said and chatted on to Mrs. Ilyush-kaya.

The bell rang. Mrs. Linou gaped at her watch in dismay. How could break be over already, and she hadn't even touched her coffee? The bell over the door rang again. In all the hubbub Apostolis couldn't make out if it was for him or for the subaltern.

"For you," said the subaltern, reblocking his ears.

And Apostolis, leaving the timetable in the hands of the Russian amazon, shot through the door on the double.

The orderly room was at the far end of the long narrow corridor, negotiating which at this hour of the day required pluck. The corridor was jammed with officers. Some standing erect drinking coffee, smoking, or eating. Others propped against the wall trying to bone up on the next lesson. There were only two lamps all told, and these, stuck like artichokes in what looked like large zinc plates, cast their light upward. Crowns and stars glinted in the penumbra. On the wall hooks hung kepis, two or three with braided peaks, above a rank of identical three-quarter-length fur-lined coats that further restricted passage through the narrow cor-ridor.

Hardly had he closed the common-room door behind him when he tripped over Captain "Goody-Goody" Agathos, who'd requested him, unbeknownst to the others, to tell him his grades.

"Nothing as yet, Captain, sir," Apostolis informed him in code, sliding adroitly between the backs of Lieutenant "Dynamite" Dinikouris and Warrant Officer "Meatball" Yialantzes.

"I'm waiting," said Goody-Goody, turning his head aside lest he arouse the suspicions of his brother officers.

Pushing and shoving, Apostolis cleared a path like an icebreaker. Percy, "Dum-Dum," and "The Booze" formed an impassable wall halfway down the corridor where it was darkest, falling midway between the two lamps. With an "excuse me," he sundered their wall, but, in turning aside, The Booze stumbled against "Chicken Shit" and spilled his coffee. Incensed, Chicken Shit swung around to see who was shoving. At the sight of the private, the blood boiled in his brain, as if he were thinking, Agh, if I just had you back at battalion, but he said nothing because soldiers at the Center had special privileges. You didn't dare even breathe on them. Which was why most of the officer-pupils suffered from inertia, deprived as they were here of the rare joy of giving orders while still having others hovering over their heads giving them orders. Apostolis had long since noticed how fresh and lively they arrived from their battalions after the fresh air of field maneuvers and how in no time at all they wilted, sagged, withered, lost their gusto and their bearings, became dazed, as if the sultry air circulating through this rectangular cul-de-sac of a building known as the "Military Stock Exchange" were actually stifling them. And in every new batch several of the "toughest," who couldn't stand this quenching of their ego, requested "suspension of their further education. . . ."

Negotiating rocks, reefs, and icebergs, he at last found himself by the door bearing the signboard ORDERLY ROOM. But beside it hung the notice board, with a knot of officers jostling for a look at the new duty roster and blocking all access. Those in back stood on tiptoe, calling on those in front to tell them which days they were on duty. "Sunday again!" he heard someone groan nearby. Seeing then that every courteous bid for break-through was foredoomed, he didn't hesitate to jab an elbow into the bulging guts of Major "Fats" Pitsigavdakis, and thrust his fist through the sudden vacuum to grab the doorknob like a drowning rat. He gave a shove, but they wouldn't open up inside. Pounding like a demon, he at last heard the hoarse tones of "Hoarse":

"Who is it?"

" 'S me, jerk, Apostolis! Open up!"

"By yourself?"

"Yeah."

And the door opened just sufficiently for him to squeeze through. A captain wanting to call his wife tried to make the most of the opportunity, but as soon as Apostolis was inside, Hoarse grated "off limits," and deftly slammed the door.

The adjutant's order was cut and dried: officer-pupils are barred from the orderly room during breaks. Because the adjutant's buddies were plagued with hangers-on, previously adjutants in different units, ever yearning for the orderly-room atmosphere, for the sight of protocols and figures and orders, for the very feel of the knobs of the stampers . . . But they were a hindrance to the permanent personnel, for work at the Center was urgent and unceasing. Interpreters came and went daily, and the CO kept issuing orders countermanding other orders, timetables canceling previous timetables. These days, especially, everyone was on his toes because, according to the CO's circular to all section leaders, "In the near future experts from the Undersecretariat of the U.S. Defense Department proposed to visit the Center to inspect the method of instruction in American Military Usage." Hence there was no room for exceptions.

"We'll also collaborate with firms abroad. Everything in our limited company will rest on secrecy," Apostolis heard on entry. The adjutant was addressing a couple of orderlies wearing grins of anticipation. Eleni was reading a thesaurus behind her typewriter. Her legs were hidden under a sheet of blue wrapping paper which covered her desk, as a result of another of the CO's orders, to keep the men from ogling. . . .

"My letter to our ambassador in Brussels will secure us the demolition materials on the Greek front at least. . . ."

"Who wanted me?" Apostolis cut in.

"CO," the adjutant informed him lackadaisically, lost to the world in dreams of tycoonery. "Smarten yourself up a bit," he added, dropping the cord of the Venetian blind.

Apostolis hitched up his pants, ran his fingers through his hair, took a furtive peek at Eleni, and knocked on the door.

"See here! That's Greece for you," exclaimed the CO the moment Apostolis entered his presence. "Four months now the typewriters we ordered have been in customs. Another four for the order to be issued, that's eight. Six months they'll lie rotting in the depot, eighteen. With a bit of luck we'll have 'em next year. In the meantime the tutors keep griping. Russians, Albanians. How are they supposed to type their texts out of context?"

Apostolis listened at attention. He hadn't the faintest notion why he'd been summoned or what the CO was talking about. He'd long since made a habit of not asking. He watched the unbroken heap of ash piling up in the ashtray in the groove of which rested the CO's black cigarette holder, the cigarette smoldering idly away. It was flanked by the whole range of Bic colored pens which served the CO for his various signatures. There was a knock, and Babis shot in like a flash, whisked away the empty coffee cup, and left a full one in its place on the saucer.

"That's Greece today for you," the CO resumed the moment they were alone. "That's why Communism marches on. It finds us fast asleep and rears up, coiling, climbing. . . ."

His nervous hands snaked through the air like serpents. Then, as if suddenly oblivious of the soldier's presence, he took up the green pen and drew circles, dotted lines, curves, parabolas. Replacing it, he picked the red, filled the circles with crosses, interwove the shapes. From the deployed array of pens, he next selected the black and in the right-hand margin wrote "Pithia Defiled" and in the left "Lord God Made Manifest." Wavering next between orange and cherry, he finally chose the former and began scribbling $A = 1, B = 2, C = 3, D = 4, Z = 26$. Lastly with the cherry-colored pen, underneath "Pithia Defiled" and "Lord God Made Manifest," he began filling in the corresponding figures. And was lost in a labyrinth of equations.

Apostolis peered out the window. He was gratified to spot the same woman he'd been watching earlier from the common room, directly opposite now, with not even the hindrance of curtains. She was combing her hair in front of a large mirror, clad in a fluffy white bathrobe that every movement of her arm opened to reveal the black bra underneath. His gaze alternated between the woman, praying inwardly she wouldn't desert him, and the CO still engrossed in additions, subtractions, divisions, multiplications. . . .

The bell rang for the beginning of the second period. Distracted by the noise, the CO looked up.

"There you are!" he declared. "The figures speak for themselves. From time immemorial to all times, to say nothing of half-time, the inference is, come what may, factor M cannot but happen."

"And yet," Apostolis pointed out, "it was the Russians who first discovered Sputnik."

"They discovered nothing," retorted the CO. "Finality has existed as teleological proof of phenomena from the beginning of beginnings to the creation of the cosmos. The corpuscle they launched was fated to fall under the sway of finality and hence into orbit. The law of gravity took instantaneous effect. They'd have discovered something if they'd reversed finality. But it was natural and only to be expected, in accordance with the everlasting will of God and toward the fulfillment of His grand omniscient pre-ordained plan, that it should fall into orbit round the terrestrial globe. . . ." He took a sip of coffee and lounged back in his arm-chair.

"I am, I might say, in the know," he resumed. "I have formulated a true *Weltanschauung*. Since 1897, namely since the inception of the Zionist movement, the Holy Father's Divine Universal Order of Finality has been disrupted. Ever since the reconstitution of the State of Israel, astronomers of world renown have observed periodic outbreaks of X-ray activity on the surface of the sun, with inverse polarity. The Italian astronomer Bedandi, director of the Faenza observatory, maintains that since the year of the reconstitution of the State of Israel, namely since 1947, we have entered upon a period of Cosmic Crisis. And in a communiqué issued in the monthly magazine *Supernova* under the title 'Natural Disasters and the Deluge of Conan Doyle,' we read that the formidable hurricanes in northwestern Europe and the recent earthquakes that continue to convulse the Mediterranean countries are the result. . . . Tonight"—his voice suddenly dropped an octave—"at seven-thirty sharp in the Parnassus hall, a lecture is being given under the aegis of the Society of Friends of New Israel. You'll be there, in plain clothes. I want you to keep your ears open and report to me first thing tomorrow morning. I may be there myself. But you're to pretend you don't know me. Above all, not a word to anyone that I sent you. . . ."

"But—"

"That's an order," he said, forestalling Apostolis. "Besides, if you don't believe me, see for yourself!" He opened his desk drawer, rummaged through some files, and drew out a sheet of paper.

"This explains why, come what may, factor M cannot but happen.

"Now you understand," the CO explained, "why no one must

know I sent you. The spirit of evil, in time of affliction, has joined in pursuit of me."

Cigarette after cigarette piled ash upon ash. He gulped down the last dregs of his coffee. Apostolis was beginning to tire of his enforced regulation stance. He gazed across at the woman, who was now donning her skirt. In the brief respite during which the CO rang the bell and ordered Hoarse to go and get him a morning paper, "crisp and fresh," Apostolis ogled the woman, who seemed to have noticed without being the least bit bothered.

"The newspapers write daily," the CO began as soon as Hoarse had fled, clutching his drachma and a half, "of the conflict that exists between America and Russia. Which is what everybody believes. Whereas the truth is there's been but one conflict and one alone, all along, since the creation of the cosmos, from the beginning of beginnings: the conflict between Judaism and Hellenism. The Jews today rule the world. They occupy the highest positions, the vital spots. They've infiltrated everywhere, all states, all systems, all governments. America and Russia are sister countries because, in both, Jews occupy the supreme strategic posts. And the Jews act in conspiracy. Unfortunately, it's all play-acting, putting on shows for the general public. Eisenhower, Khrushchev, Adenauer, Macmillan, they're all in the cast. They quarrel, make believe, play different roles according to the times, while the prompter remains the same. And the prompter is the Jew. It's no coincidence, the fact that the inspiration behind the Zionist movement was a critic, journalist, and playwright. Or that he conceived this idea of a theater. And Spyros Melas, who's being groomed for president of the Academy, has exactly the same qualifications as the founder of Zionism: critic, journalist, playwright. Ardent Jew lover. Moreover, in Greece today, all of 'em, government and opposition, the lot, they're all agents for the Jews. That's why we're fast going to the devil. Venizelos was of Jewish extraction. With Max Nordau he planned the Judaization of Greece via Communism. Why did they house the refugees from Asia Minor around

the palaces and mansions of our civic centers? So that with the
wealth of others in full view they'd more willingly convert to
Communist maggots for the elimination of our race. Why weren't
they dispersed around the villages, where they'd become nationalists? . . . How many pints of water did you splash over your
face?" he asked him curtly, catching Apostolis in mid-yawn.

"I have washed, sir," blurted Apostolis, slamming to attention.

"I didn't ask you if you'd washed. I asked you how many pints
of water you splashed on your face."

"But how could I keep count, sir?"

"For the sake of argument, let's call it two and a half pints
splashed. Now run along and splash on another half."

"But—"

"That's an order. Scat!"

Apostolis made for the door, only to see it open abruptly and
the adjutant hurtle in like a whirlwind.

"Sir," he began in a tremulous squeak, "we've just had the list
of new interpreters due to report tomorrow."

"Well?" said the CO, lighting a fresh cigarette.

"Among the names," stammered the adjutant, "there's one that
sounds . . . I mean, not just sounds . . . Cohen Benjamin."

"Shut the door," the CO instantly commanded Apostolis, who
was right beside it. Then smirked meaningfully. And suddenly
paled.

"What is he?" he inquired, feigning indifference. "Enlisted man
or subaltern?"

"Subaltern, sir," replied the adjutant, glancing down the list of
names.

The pair of them had the air of conspirators. So the adjutant was
also "in the know," was privy to the inexorable battle of Hellenism
versus Judaism. He'd once drafted the report to Ben-Gurion,
premier of Israel, in which the CO demanded a retrial of Christ.
And Apostolis recalled in the old days, when he first came to the
Center, a similar case had arisen. The victim at that time was an
enlisted man, Benveniste by name, from Salonika. He'd not even

handed his marching orders to the adjutant when the CO, who'd been waiting since the day before, shot out of his office, snorted and sniffed him over, and in two shakes slapped him in the cells for ten days, on a charge of having "one or more buttons unbuttoned." The soldier was nonplused. What a reception on his first day in a new unit! When he dared to open his mouth, he forthwith got twenty days, on a charge of "insubordination." A subaltern took him to one side and explained the peculiar circumstances with reference to the CO. He even warned him, if he had any pull, not to hesitate to use it, as the CO had no intention of stopping there in his persecution, because he believed he was himself being persecuted by the Jews. (Swastikas, convex earth, ice eternally at war with fire. Ino, my brother! There, in the crematoria, could you have known the spirit of Hitler would live on?) That same afternoon Apostolis happened to be on duty with Goody-Goody. About six they were confronted in the orderly room by a thickset man, wearing a felt Homburg pulled low over his eyes, who introduced himself as a colonel from intelligence and asked for the commanding officer who'd so mercilessly punished Benveniste. They gave him his home address, and the colonel went off threatening eternal damnation. Next day the CO slunk in like a whipped dog. He told the adjutant the sentence was commuted to detention. At eleven he reduced it to "confined to barracks." And at three, before going home, Apostolis—stationed by the door, with his briefcase bulging with bones for the dog, ready to dash off and reserve him a seat on the Syntagma–Papagos bus—heard him tell the adjutant that "The powers of darkness opposed to the Divine Will are seeking to thwart the holy crusade for the destruction of the seed of Abraham."

"I fail to see," he was saying now in the same embittered tones, "why you're so preoccupied with this matter, when there are Jews everywhere today, and the government even promotes them to the rank of officers. What goes right in Greece today for one to wonder at one thing going wrong? The typewriters in customs for six months. President of the Academy the spitting image of the founder of Zionism. Comrade Kazantzakis declares 'we're just like the Jews.' Well, let him come. We'll take care of him as best we can, since we serve the fatherland that serves the Jews who today rule the world. . . ."

"You mean you want to—" the adjutant began.

"I want nothing," he silenced him. "I have long since said my piece. The significant disturbances in the solar mass will result in Cosmic Crisis. It's clear as daylight that only a Helleno-Christian hegemony can save the world. Otherwise, the shifting of our planet's isothermic zones and the melting of the polar icecaps consequent upon this shift will result in the submersion of the seaboard cities of every continent and a probable jolt to the earth's axis. A word to the wise, you know, a nod's as good as a wink. Cohen, you say?"

"Yessir. 'Cohen Benjamin, son of Isaac and Ruth,' " the adjutant quoted from the list.

The CO stood up, looked about him like a trapped beast.

"Order a cease-teaching in all sections, all officers to assemble in Room G5. Dismissed."

"But what's going on? What for this time?" Mr. Donias whined at the adjutant.

"I'd just set my darling little dears some tests," wailed Mrs. Ilyushkaya.

"There must be a reason," Mr. Patsakov assured them, ever anxious to keep in with the CO so as to chalk up a little extra overtime on the official general-staff timetable.

Meanwhile, the officers had begun to congregate in Room G5, many with pads at the ready to take notes.

"May we attend the briefing?" Mrs. Linou inquired.

"Top secret," the adjutant told her and, to elude the mob of tutors suddenly inundating the orderly room, started dictating to Eleni: "Submitted herewith the enclosed memorandum of traveling expenses incurred by reserve officers of DEA . . ."

And Eleni sang:

DEA, IDEA, Ideal,
tomb and coffin—
Kitzikis Michael, son of Anastasios and Penelope,
Chouvardas Emmanuel, son of Paul and Antiope,
Zacharias Zacharias, son of Zacharias and Zacharia,
Mavroyenis Pericles, son of Nikos and Maria.

"All DEA reservists entitled to ten days' additional subsistence . . ."

> Stance [she sang],
> life's dance,
> letters A to Z,
> iron fingers,
> mourning bands,
> Saint Demetrius is dead.

"Taking into account the NATO maneuvers' code name, ALEXANDER THE GREAT, those DEA reservists stationed in barracks should —no, strike that and write . . ."

> I strike out and write,
> Patsakov's sighs,
> for Ilyushkaya's thighs,
> which Donias denies,
> to the boys, to the guys,
> who must button their flies,
> lest rivers arise,
> and drown me in eyes,
> while the light from the dynamo,
> degenerates and dies,
> all my days at the school of
> Foreign Languages . . .
>
> The recipient

False Windows

The evening of the kick marked a turning point in our friendship. True, until then I'd always been "under" my friend, more like his aide-de-camp or a satellite. As my senior in years, he'd taken me under his wing, cared for me, kept an eye on me, without holding me in check. And at the time, I needed him. When I saw him in the evening, after a hectic day, I felt the severity of his mien suffuse me like a potion, soothing and softening my spikes. It was like drinking a cup of hot camomile. And he had a way of asserting his authority without making me feel at all dependent. When we went out in the evening to eat at Stratis' or to see a movie, it was always he who paid, in a manner so natural that I never felt in the least beholden. And I always knew that my being with him had no strings attached. His was the knack of people who live alone yet keep devoted friends.

I, however, entertained quite other visions of a relationship. I craved intensity, passion, dynamism. While I shared with him all my inmost thoughts, my anxieties, my longings, he told me none of his secrets. He was most niggardly in confidence, which sometimes made me feel a complete stranger in his company. "The stars rule a world of their own," he'd once told me, to which I replied that stars collide, shift position in space, vanish from the sky. The blood seethed in my veins, and the museumlike tranquillity reigning over his countenance had, I must admit, begun to irritate me. I needed a smack in the ear to wake me up, not a caress that would lull me into slumber.

On one occasion, for instance, when I was in full and avid flight because of my girl friend, I told him how my eyes beheld her like a flower, how I drank her every word like holy water. I said that of course we hadn't yet reached the stage of consummating our relationship, and that it didn't really bother me, because from what little we did I could imagine plenty; so from the plenty I imagined,

I desired little in reality. We always parted to meet again, and always met once more to part. I drank and smoked heavily, my nerves were taut as hawsers, and while I was on the verge of tears telling him all this, I was flabbergasted to hear him suggest, in the coolest possible manner, that I feel her up more often so she'd come around of her own accord. At such moments his *sang-froid* froze me rigid. I found our coexistence utterly incompatible. He could never understand me. What did I hope to gain from him? And choking with a wave of sudden rage I started accusing him, finding every fault: he's cold, thick-skinned, hypocritical, impotent in love . . . he's . . . he's. . . . But for all I pushed, he wouldn't topple. After all the pitching and tossing I suffered at the hands of others, what joy it was to tumble back of an evening into the sequestered vale of his unruffled calm! It struck you like the stillness of the church when you've just left a demonstration.

What proved the cause of our separation I shall state later. I wish now to speak of our friendship, of what formed its backbone. My friend and I had another Friend, an absent Friend who bound us like brothers in our constant need to talk about Him. That His absence was the conjoining link in our own friendship was confirmed for me on another occasion, when the three of us were together—my friend, our Friend, and I. He'd come to see us, as a guest at my friend's home. Never had we been so mutually alien, so hostile, as if His coming had caused a sudden rift between us. We each wanted Him to the exclusion of the other. For heaven's sake, why can't you go away and leave us alone for a while? my friend's glance seemed to imply. But I knew Him first, mine retorted. And I asked our Friend something about a time my friend knew nothing of. So we were constantly at loggerheads, with neither of us in the mood to give way. But when our Friend—whom, to avoid confusion, I shall henceforth call our Idol—left and we found ourselves once more alone, we dashed at each other in our yearning for Him, forever idealizing Him, singing His praises, mimicking His speech, His movements, and in the end so beatifying Him in imagination that, had He but heard us from some hidden recess, He'd surely have died laughing. Ordinary folk like my friend and me have need of Idols, to appear in our own eyes more important. Like the strength the faithful draw by reflection from the God they put their faith in.

It would have been a simple matter if it had ended there. But our Idol also wrote music. He sent us manuscripts of His compositions, which my friend would play on the piano. And I, unable to play a note, lent a limp ear. Deep down I knew it gave him a sadistic kick to initiate me into the music of our Idol, to decipher its codes for me. But then, he'd never play unless I asked first. He awaited my supplication. And being less in control of my emotions, choking with nostalgia for the Idol, I implored him, every time, to play for me. Then he'd get up as if at great cost, while deep down I knew he was ablaze with the same desire, and with languid motion bend his steps toward the piano—his limbs, you'd think from the way he walked, divested utterly of time—and sit down on the revolving piano stool, where those stalactites of his serenity that were his long, sensitive fingers would melt over the ivories, drenching the room with melody and dissolving our hearts in yearning.

This always happened after hours of prating about our Idol. He was our favorite theme; His name tasted infinitely sweet upon our lips. But words are like brooks; they sometimes run dry. Then, as I say, their place was taken by the warble of bird song. Followed once more by the babble of the brook. Between awarbling and ababbling, in a pastoral paradise, we passed our days, our weeks, and our months.

The only trouble was that the music sheets wore out with overuse. Trills and embellishments faded. My friend, who had a weak memory—one of the reasons for his never becoming a concert pianist—could no longer play them. This for the first time made us equals. I'd sit beside him and whistle the tunes while he tried to revive them on the keyboard. Our Idol had meanwhile gone abroad for further studies, leaving us forever starved of His music.

Was it, I wonder, divine providence or mere coincidence that during this critical period of our friendship, His music came out on a record? A major Italian recording company had issued an LP of His best pieces, with a picture of our Idol on the sleeve, the same picture we each had in our rooms. We rushed out to buy the record, which we played on an old gramophone until by and by the LP, too, got worn out and scratched, the needle jumped the worn grooves, and we tired of paying for our nostalgia with the same old coin. . . .

We were in danger of having nothing to say to each other. In vain we sought new stations on the radio. The radio, like the piano, was in sad repair. We could tune in only Greek stations. And so long as we weren't caught up with our Idol, I, for one, felt we really had nothing more to say. I tried coming to grips with him over some question or other, at last confronting him face to face, but he found all such duologue trivial, a waste of time, and, with art and artifice, always managed to persuade me we had no cause for dispute. In other words, that you might understand and vindicate me—though that's the last thing I crave of the reader—I must say that I'd verily become a pawn in his hands, a pawn he moved as he chose, to whatever square he chose. I suddenly realized this one evening in the European Youth Movement Club while watching him play his favorite game. With such serenely masterful fingers did he move pawns, bishop, knights, queen, that his opponent, smoking with nervous desperation, kept losing his head and retreating, until my friend, devoid of any spark of aggression, had reduced him to such a hopeless position that finding the sight of his king in check more than he could bear, with a swipe he wiped the chessboard clean. I saw myself, as I say, as a pawn in my friend's hands and, behaving in like manner, gave our so-called friendship a good kick in order to make my escape.

When at length he came after me, I felt compelled to speak my mind, to spell out the truth in no uncertain terms: I'd no taste at all for the insular, monotonous life we led; surely there were much more interesting things to spend our time on; there was fun to be had; rock 'n' roll had just made its first appearance here, and its rhythms roused youth to a frenzy; after all, in our day and age historic events were in progress and we couldn't go on ad infinitum masturbating in public over Salvator de Madariaga's succulent fantasies of a united Europe—which would be more a bunch of grapes than a bowl of peaches, since all the states would hang like grapes from the same branch, with none of the mutual independence of peaches—while in private languishing over an out-of-tune piano playing the worn-out melodies of our émigré Idol.

"You're right," he said. "We've burned our bridges."

We were sitting in my room. He picked up the letter opener from my desk and stared first at one end, then at the other.

"Me, too," he resumed after a pause, dropping the letter opener, "I'm sick of this life. I'm thinking of going to Zanzibar. I have relatives there. . . . We'll see," he added, as if the very thought of a likely change wearied him.

No, I knew full well he had no intention of going. He was too settled here, with his bachelor flat and acquaintance of long standing with the rhythm of everyday life, Saturday night and Sunday morning sin—peace doesn't come easy in this world. And I knew from what he'd said that things hadn't always been this way. He'd dreamed of studying, of going abroad. But the guerrilla war, hardship, family obligations had pinned him down here, and now it was too late. He'd missed the boat. So many cheated feelings, so many shipwrecked dreams had compounded a hard shell around him, a carapace, his only defense. What he'd just said about going to Africa he no more believed than I did. It had merely come back to him at that moment like a distant echo from the past, as an endemic bird, left behind by a migrating flock and seeing formations of other birds on the wing, recalls his origins. . . . And then I felt sorry for him. Perhaps I shouldn't have done it, I know, but it was something beyond my control. Compassion overwhelmed me, some unconscious impulse made me lean forward, across lawbooks, across codes, bonds, equities, and touch his hand.

"You're the only friend I've got," I whispered huskily.

I watched him watching me with that deep mysterious gaze of his, while in those dark caves that were his eyes I saw with joy and anguish a flicker of something struggling toward the light. His eyes were gleaming now, gleaming weirdly, as if cleansed of dust, of time. They were warm. I felt their warmth for the first time on my skin, and I was glad. The words I'd just uttered seemed to have found a chink by which to enter, to touch him. The armor he wore wasn't quite sealed. One slit, one tiny invisible slit was left open in the hope that someday some human tissue might slip through and warm him. I'd withdrawn my hand from his, thinking, or feeling, all this, when I saw the flame in his eyes fading, little by little, as it had kindled, a last spark lingering in the pupils, until that, too, was lost in darkness. His eyes had regained their usual expression, become once more cold and inaccessible, ever ready to avoid you. Then—it was like watching a robot—I saw his hand, his fine, sensitive hand rise and move toward me. Implausible, animallike, it advanced through the air, traversed the corner of the table, and landed smoothly on my knee. His arm now united us like an aerial bridge erected by the Royal Engineers, in that it had been totally engineered. And I saw the vast vacuum this gesture masked. A form without content, a form charming enough on the surface but which failed to deceive me, for I recalled an architectural oddity I'd seen on the old mansions of Pelion. These had once had real fanlights, but the peasants bricked them up, painting on the fresh masonry under the eaves where the real windows had once been, now just their shape—as elegant and refined as a sketch by Matisse, and known in the folk art of the region by the name "false windows."

Swings and Merry-go-rounds

"I'm afraid, Mr. Ioannides," the young assistant in the travel agency informed me, "your passport isn't ready."

"But you promised me today—" I started to say, in protest.

"I'm well aware of what I promised, but there have been unforeseen snags."

And snapping shut his briefcase full of other people's passports, he leaned forward so the girl operating the nearby adding machine couldn't hear. "You must . . ." He hesitated. "Better discuss it outside."

We threaded our way through a crowd of foreigners and Greeks, he in front, I trailing. I asked, "It couldn't be my tax declaration, could it?"

"No, no."

"Or some hang-up with my voting record? I told you, I didn't vote in the last elections because . . ."

"Your passport, Mr. Ioannides," he told me, once clear of the agency, "is ready, but you must collect it in person from the Security Department, Section G5, Room 32, Inspector Plangas."

That shook me. He, too, felt ill-at-ease. I could see him fiddling nervously with the handle of his briefcase, avoiding my eye.

"Had I known beforehand," he said, "that you had dealings with Security I should not have unduly inconvenienced you. I'd have started from there. Whereas now, that's where we've wound up, with no knowing if all our efforts haven't been in vain. . . ."

"But I haven't applied to go east," I objected.

"That's irrelevant. It's a mere formality. Of no special significance."

Well might he wish to enlarge on the subject of political views, though clearly he desisted out of tact. To his way of thinking, a man's opinions were as personal as his taste in women. You can't say the woman I love is ugly, because by the very fact that I love her, for me she ceases to be ugly.

"What do I owe you?" I asked in conclusion.

"Oh, nothing, nothing at all."

"What d'you mean, nothing? What about the price of the wire to the draft board?"

"Charged to the agency."

"And all your foot-slogging from Tax Office to Security?"

"Dutybound to be of service to our clients."

"But—"

"But me no buts. When you have your passport, just drop by and show me."

And he dashed off with the other passports he had stashed in his briefcase.

I stepped into a barbershop for a quick shave. I didn't want to go before the inspector looking like a tramp. The barber asked me if I'd like a trim. Checking the time, I decided to have the trim to give myself a brief respite. Though for every second I spent in the barber's chair, staring at my face in the mirror, doubts gnawed at me as to what on earth Security could want with me. What had I done of late to rouse their suspicion suddenly? I'd inherited no record, so to speak. My father had always been a nationalist and my grandfather, on my father's side, a village cop. On my mother's side there could be no problem because she was born abroad. As for me, apart from my somewhat progressive leanings, known only to my closest friends, I'd never given them cause to deem me suspect. I avoided politics at the office, was even a reserve officer in the army. Could one of my "close" friends be a stoolie for the fuzz? I recoiled at the very thought, causing the barber to back off abruptly. He was just resoaping my other cheek and advised me to avoid quick movements. Or maybe it was the letter I'd written to a friend of mine in Paris recounting the details of the Lambrakis assassination? But the right to confidential correspondence is guaranteed by the Constitution. I asked the barber for confirmation of this, but he shook his head skeptically.

"The law's one thing, what happens is another," he replied.

Then all of a sudden I remembered something and wondered that I hadn't thought of it before. In the office, a month ago, I was chatting to a colleague about the new statue of Truman. We'd mentioned the pleats in his tails, the surrounding pool of water, as well as the fact that it was badly sited—it ought to face the avenue instead of the apartment houses opposite. "And you know, Costa," I'd said, "the unveiling was held on the day of Lambrakis' funeral." And right on cue I heard the voice of our personnel officer—whom hitherto I hadn't noticed at the door—chime in with, "That'll do. It's not your job to prattle about art." And he stomped out. Yet the fact that he had said "art" and not "politics" now had me worried. At last I was beginning to pick up the threads, to connect one apparently unconnected fact with another. I paid and stepped out.

I specially selected a taxi bigger than the rest to make a good impression at the entrance to Security. But the taxi couldn't stop where I'd intended because two other cars were parked in front. Thus deprived of the glory with which I'd desired to violate the sanctuary, I paid and walked the rest of the way.

At the door, contrary to expectation, they didn't ask me what I was after. I was already on the first floor, lost in the murk of that loathsome building, by the time I noticed a button missing from my pants. Rather, it wasn't the first time I'd noticed it; it was the first time it had bothered me. Before one's judges one must always appear impeccable, self-confident, and assured, with no petty infringements of regulation dress and bearing to aggravate feelings of guilt.

Thus I mounted the stairs, my heart in my mouth and all my attention riveted on the missing button, surrounded by people scurrying up and down: women, old folk, small children. Only the presence of the coffee vendor reassured me. A familiar element in the midst of all the offices, something like the relief an astronaut might feel at finding the root of a tree on the moon's surface. Be that as it may, I'd forgotten to ask where Section G5 and Room 32 were. Back I went down to the first floor. There I found the office I was seeking, and also, Inspector Plangas, on the phone to some superior, judging by the expression of eager servility which, the second the receiver was back on the hook, he flung into the waste-paper basket like a disposable mask, only to assume a snotty air to question the pregnant woman in front of him. I'd just joined the line waiting to see the inspector when a plain-clothes officer did me the courtesy of asking me what I wanted.

"My passport," I responded in a proud, disdainful tone, as if I knew the whole farce backward.

"Go first to Room A7 on the third floor, then come back here," he instructed.

I went up to the third, then returned to the first, and then from first floor to second—with a constant supply of slips of paper inscribed with code numbers—finally to wind up in the basement in a labyrinth of passages jam-packed with files. I reflected, cigarette in hand (there being no one to tell me "no smoking"), what a savior for the long-suffering Greek race its smoldering butt would prove if dropped, by accident, right in the middle. I was proceeding through this tunnel that seemed as endless as human misery, when a dead end brought me to an abrupt halt. The passage went no farther. Just a couple of offices opening off to right and left, exactly as I remembered the end of the gallery in the Belgian coal mine, over 3,000 feet down, opening onto an entire railway station, complete with rails, signals, and stationmaster. Someone who seemed to pull some weight, to judge by the alacrity with which the assistant served him, passed ahead of me. My sojourn in this navel of black solitude would've been unbearable were it not for the transistor music echoing from the office next door, to the right. At long last my turn came, I handed over the slip issued to me in the office with the wooden railing, and the assistant went off to rummage through the overloaded shelves. I saw him waver between two dossiers. He tugged out the fatter one, bulging with what must have been at least 500 convictions, toted it back to his office, and opened it. I was shocked to see my own name, Evangelos Ioannides, son of Panayotis, handwritten, and over it a faded stamp DECEASED. I looked at the man, who was now staring at me aghast. He took up the slip again, compared the code numbers, found they matched, and grinned.

"There must've been some mistake," he said. Then, tearing a sheet from his pad, he scribbled, "Lacks record." "Now take this to Inspector Plangas so you can collect your passport," he instructed.

I could have kissed him. With the elation of the diver surfacing after a lung-bursting plunge into the depths of the ocean, I thrashed panting and gasping up to the first floor. For all that, I was irked by this "lacks." Why couldn't he have scrawled a short and sweet "Okay" or "No file" or "Not known"? This "lacks" made me feel more suspect, convinced me that by the grace and favor of some deceased fraternal benefactor, or malefactor, I must obtain a record.

"So you're lacking," chortled the inspector, twirling the slip through his fingers. "We'll have to see about you."

"What are you driving at?" I demanded, obviously rattled.

"You a Communist?"

"I don't see what your question has to do with my case."

"All right, all right," he said, taking his pencil from its case and jotting something on a piece of paper. "We'll have ample opportunity to discuss it some other time." He handed me the piece of paper, adding, *"Bon voyage."*

I took it, thanked him, and as soon as I was out of the office stopped to examine it. "Permission to travel abroad," it said. With his signature at the bottom. Completely at a loss, with no passport, there I stood pondering the implications of all this hassle, when the same plain-clothes cop, seated opposite the inspector's office, accosted me with the words, "You can pick up your passport at the Ministry of the Interior. It'll be forwarded straight from here. Though it might get held up in ministry procedure, so I'll come along and make sure you get it today."

His sudden alacrity made me doubly distressed. "That's very kind of you," I replied, "but tomorrow'll do."

"No, it's not right you should lose precious days off your vacation," he insisted. "So I'll come along."

I was troubled in the first place by the fact that he knew I was on vacation. And on top of that, it's not easy to tell a security cop he's not wanted.

"It's Italy you're going to, isn't it?" he asked me as we left the building together.

"Yes," I said. "Rome via Brindisi."

He scowled. We were right by the door, outside, the guards saluting him. Passing by with his tray, the coffee boy mentioned something about an order.

"Forget it," growled the cop.

The light of day, to which I'd looked for redemption after this nose dive into the night of Security, now stung my eyes like a thousand spotlights zeroed in on me to force a confession. But confession of what? My best move, of course, would be to take a cab. But who knows, even the cabs in the adjacent taxi stand might just be a cover. So I preferred to leg it. Besides, the ministry wasn't far. Quarter of an hour. And it was still only eleven.

I then sized him up for the first time. He had a mustache, eyes heavily charged with confidential documents, lips tight-sealed with the stamp of secrecy, hands of a karate black belt. What did he want of me? What was he after? I'd have given my Christmas bonus to know. The fatal "refrain" echoed through my mind: "And you know, Costa, the unveiling was held the day of Lambrakis' funeral." The personnel officer stood before me—how did such an incompetent bungler get to be personnel officer, if he hadn't some reason for being there? He had a mustache just like this guy's, and the same brooding gaze.

He fell into step beside me. I felt every head in the street turn and stare at me, as if to be thus escorted automatically rendered me suspect. At Stournara we turned left on Kaningos. I prayed inwardly I'd run into some acquaintance, stop for a chat, and shake off this nightmare. But with strangers on all sides I was bound

not for the Ministry of the Interior, but to appear before some
higher judge to answer why I lacked a record. It was more than
I could take, and at the next corner I suggested a drink. He con-
sented, though not for himself. He'll take it as a bribe, I thought.
The café had pinball machines, one-armed bandits, table football.
A sign read, BLASPHEME YE NOT. BY ORDER OF THE MANAGEMENT.

"Married?"

"No," he said. "Engaged."

"Earn much?"

"My fiancée has a dress shop."

"I'm from Thessaly," I said. "Farsala."

"From North Epirus myself," he said. "Koritsa."

FEELING BLUE? THEN THE PINBALL'S FOR YOU.

"Chinese in Albania," I said. "Not Russians."

"Chinese, Russians," he said, "what's the difference?"

NO WRITING ON THE BILLIARD TABLES WITH THE CUES. NO SHOUTING.
NO SINGING. NO ROWDYISM.

"Your passport'll be there by now," he said. "If you want it
today, best not delay."

I stood up. Paid. And off we went once more.

Then he said, "My face is too familiar, so we better split up. You
walk fifty yards ahead; I'll follow. We'll meet up at the entrance."

This we did. He let me draw ahead, then followed. True, I did
think of giving him the slip, around the next corner and away in
the maze of narrow streets in the heart of Athens. But where
would I go? I didn't want them coming after me at home. I
intended keeping the whole story to myself as far as possible,
because I knew not what was yet to come. Which was precisely
what worried me. Why was this cop on my tail? "You a Communist?" Extraordinary question. Since my namesake was deceased.
Some coincidence! Smoking like a chimney, I was swept across
intersections amid waves of people. Until I arrived at the entrance
to the ministry, and there he stood waiting.

The locked door was besieged by a jostling mob of men and
women emerging from the adjoining emigration bureau to wait by

the impassable gatekeeper's folding grill. But when the cop flashed his ID they let us straight in. The crowd's howl of protest at this gross exception descended like a ton of bricks on my shoulders. But what could I say? How could I turn around and tell them I'd be right out there waiting alongside them sooner than have this curse of an escort on my neck!

The passport section was on the second floor, and likewise besieged by a mob jostling as before the icon of the Holy Virgin. But the miracle was a long time coming.

"I've got friends upstairs," he told me. "I'll hurry along there and speed things up with your passport. Don't budge an inch."

I waited. He went up and down three or four times before finally informing me the passport was in the hands of the proper official.

"But before we part," he added, "there's something I'd like to ask you."

At last, I thought, here comes the crunch. Now he's going to ask me to sign some declaration, now. . . . But anything would be better than this sickening suspense, this slow roasting over the embers of anguish.

"Let's go over there. We might be overheard." He looked somber, grim. He stood me in the corner. When he felt sure we were beyond earshot, he slid his hand into his inside pocket and pulled out his wallet. "My card," he said. "And 200 drachs."

"But—"

"Keep your voice down. I know it's against the rules, but I wanted to ask you a favor. . . . In Brindisi you can buy these big dolls, you know, popeyed, surprised-looking, just like women. Well, my fiancée's been begging me to get somebody to bring her one of these dolls. It's the only thing she's ever asked me for. And seeing we're getting married shortly. . . . If you can get pink, all the better. If not, blue'll do. In the box, of course . . . She'll have the surprise of her life. . . . Cost about 200 drachs . . . I'd be really obliged. And next time you need anything, just call on me. About how long'll I need to wait?"

"I'll be back in ten days," I said, taking the money and the card.

"Oh, thanks, thanks a million," he said squeezing my hand. "I thought from the start you'd be willing. When I saw you in the inspector's office I said to myself, 'He looks like a good guy, I'll ask him. And if he refuses, he won't go and rat on me.' We're shit-scared of informers, too, you know. There's ratting everywhere—scares us more than does ordinary folks. . . . Thanks a million. You'll work wonders for our wedding. Have a good trip. See you soon."

And I watched him skip down the ministry stairs two at a time.

Beauteous Edessa
Conservation Society

"Your Reverence," He began, "my lord High Sheriff, General, sir, Mister Mayor, Mister Public Prosecutor, most worthy fellow citizens, ladies and gentlemen, the reason we are gathered here tonight is well known to all of us. May I be permitted, however, a brief recap of this affair which has long been hanging, like the sword of Damocles, over our heads, rather, over our beautiful city, historic Edessa, that has so generously contributed in the past toward the bloody liberation of Macedonia."

Faint applause echoed from the back of the hall. He was speaking without notes. He took a sip of water.

"Well, the subject, as you know," He resumed, "is the waterfalls. Yes. The pride of our city, which they wish, we hear, in the name of electricity, to decapitate. I shall not venture upon the technical details of the problem. Though when our society's general committee delegated to me the responsibility of tonight's address to you, our town's elite, I felt, I must confess, most flattered, because in my opinion we can, all of us, make some small contribution, in the measure of our means, to thwart the execution of this heinous project.

"Do I make myself clear, or should I perhaps spell out the harsh truth? We all know these falls have for centuries constituted the crowning glory of our polity, the attraction drawing tourists from home and abroad to admire, to relish, to refresh themselves in the cool shade of the lofty plane trees in the square, which, like a hanging Babylonian terrace, dominates the plain. How then, let me ask you, can these vandals wish, so unashamedly, to butcher the splendor of our city? It's like chopping off a girl's blond ponytail. Like robbing a palm full of silver of all its wealth. And whither is this silver proffered? To our thirsting eyes, of course.

"Willows weep on the banks of the tributaries that bear water to the falls. Ducks of all species swim on the waters to within a hairsbreadth of the razor's edge. All the beauty, all the cool freshness of our city, stems precisely from these inexhaustible and ever-flowing waters welling from the womb of our poor earth to execute their leap into the void, if you'll pardon the expression, scribing thus the graph of their majestic fall.

"For the falls, ladies and gentlemen, are a natural force, a force of the earth, the tongue of our mother earth intoning her heartfelt yearning. They are like the people.

"When I say 'people,' I do not exaggerate. Our falls, our many-splendored, much-sung, rushing waterfalls constitute the instinctive outflow of a *force majeure* boiling from the bowels of the earth. So very much like the people, the mass of people flooding the squares in demonstration of their faith in an ideal. Such an onrush no barricade, no police force, no truncheon can arrest.

"A waterfall were the people of the French Revolution. A waterfall, the people of this our land who rose against the conquering Turk. How, then, can one decapitate a whole people, a force more forceful than force, a melting of the antediluvian ice lurking in the heart of each and every man?"

Two individuals seated midway down the hall got up, jammed their felt Homburgs low over their eyes, and slipped out noiselessly, unnoticed even by Him.

"It may well be," He continued, "that I've got carried away, but by what if not by the subject itself? Cast your grown minds back to younger days when we sat watching Tarzan films. Remember how when Tarzan came to the waterfall nothing could hold him back? Remember how this tamer of the jungle strove against the untamable torrent? Such a force, then, a Niagaran force has carried me away, too, me, a humble clerk in the town post office, in charge over the long years of your own 'return to sender' department.

"But though individuals may die, waterfalls are immortal. For this reason they cannot emasculate us. They cannot, in the name of electricity, under such false pretexts, chop off our balls. . . ."

The women started to leave, the bishop tapped his gilded crook in anger, the mayor eyed the sheriff, who eyed the public prosecutor.

"A slip of the tongue," He continued in a cold sweat, "I humbly beg pardon of the ladies, of all present, and crave leave to resume. . . . As I was saying, after the coup the people at last became a cataract. Nothing can hold them back. Those who believe their force will slacken are hiding their heads in the sand. We are invincible. We are the splendor of the parched Greek earth, so long-suffering in the past, so downtrodden to this very day. Those who deny the importance of the cataracts of modern-day Edessa have cataracts in their eyes. They see not. They are blind. Sightless. Let them go cringe beneath the falls, in the caves full of stalactites and stalagmites, where the bats fly in dread lest they perish in the light of day.

"Edessa without waterfalls, gentlemen, would no longer be Edessa, but something else. Greece without the people would be a negation of Greece. No mold can contain the brute force of a waterfall. No puppet government can contain a people. Down with canned food! Down with the canned breath of the Beatles on sale in the stores of London! Long live the fresh air of the Greek countryside. Long live the falls of Edessa!

"Let me continue! Don't interrupt! This isn't the Chamber! I've more to say! Much more to add! So many years a humble clerk, sleeves black to the elbows, so many years voiceless, faceless, at your beck and call, like a faithful lap dog, and now . . . *now* . . . that you've given me the chance to speak, now that we are gathered here together . . . *now* . . . let me go on. . . . I crave only the great favor you've denied me for forty years, of speaking . . . of saying the falls must stay. . . . Do not decapitate them! Don't chop off their hands! Show them, Your Reverence, my lord High Sheriff, Mister Mayor, Mister Public Prosecutor, your mercy, lest we be doomed. Even at night the falls shine white, cast light on our Erebus . . .

let me finish . . . Mister Public Prosecutor, as representative of the law, Mister Public Prosecutor . . . Mister Public Prosecutor . . ."

Three-wheeled motorcycle license number 49981 ran over the evening's speaker. The medical examination certified intracranial lesions and contusions of the cerebral stem. Clinically He was dead. But the waterfalls live on, tongue of the earth intoning her heart-felt yearning.